WALK ON

THE SPIRITUAL JOURNEY OF U2

STEVE STO

Walk On: The Spiritual Journey of U2
Published by Relevant Books, a division of Relevant Media Group, Inc.

www.relevant-books.com
www.relevantmediagroup.com

Design by Relevant Solutions
Bobby Jones, Daniel Ariza
(www.relevant-solutions.com)

Scripture quotations are from:
New American Standard Bible® (NASB) © 1960, 1977, 1995
by the Lockman Foundation. Used by permission.

Library of Congress Catalog Card Number: 2001119644
International Standard Book Number: 088419-793-X

For information:
RELEVANT MEDIA GROUP, INC.
POST OFFICE BOX 951127
LAKE MARY, FL 32795
407-333-7152

02 03 04 05 09 8 7 6 5 4 3

Printed in the United States of America

CONTENTS

ACKNOWLEDGEMENTS

Let me acknowledge first of all the genius of U2's members, who have thrilled me with their rhythms and touched me deep in my soul, and the journalists and authors whose books and articles I have mined for background and quotations and whose work on U2 is much more insightful than mine—especially Bill Flanagan, Neil McCormick, Joe Jackson, the late Bill Graham, Liam Mackey, Robert Hilburn, Steve Turner, Niall Stokes, Sean O'Hagan and John Waters.

Thanks also to my friends who have given me enthusiasm, little hints of insight or resources along the way: Tim Flaherty, Tina Murphy, William Mackay, Derek Poole, Paul Bowman, Jude Adam, Graeme Thompson, Bernie Joyce, Ian Scott, Geoff Bailie, Gordon Ashbridge, Brian Houston, Mark Houston, Chris Fry, David Dark, Rick Johnston, Stephen Orr, Lorna McMahon, Gareth Dunlop, Juliet Turner and Adrian Stewart.

More thanks than words can say to Cameron Strang and all at Relevant Media Group for taking a chance with an Irish novice they had never met. It has been an honor that I often have felt unworthy of.

Special thanks to Kyle Minor, whose fault this book is and whose patience, enthusiasm and insightful editing shaped it and made it possible. Thanks to Melissa Bogdany, who needed much patience during the final editing.

Thank you to my students who live with me in Derryvolgie Hall in Belfast; you keep me having to sharpen my faith to meet the needs of our culture.

I would like to send love to my family: to my Mum and Dad, to my in-laws and, most of all, to my long-suffering and wonderful wife, Janice, and my two incredible daughters, Caitlin and Jasmine Grace. It is over… "come, come away, my love…"

STEVE STOCKMAN – BELFAST CITY

FOREWORD
by
STEVE BEARD

As a devout Los Angeles Lakers fan, I was tuned into the first game of the 2001 NBA Championships when it was announced that U2 would be performing live during the halftime show. U2's concert was in Boston while the game was being played in Los Angeles. When the cameras switched from one venue to the other, television viewers saw Bono praying on his knees.

"What can I give back to God for the blessings he poured out on me?" he said. "I lift high the cup of salvation as a toast to our Father. To follow through on the promise I made to you." The lead singer of arguably the most popular rock band on the planet was loosely reciting a prayer from Psalm 116 on national television.

In describing U2's 2001 Elevation tour to *Rolling Stone* magazine, Bono said fans had told him they sensed "good vibrations" at the concerts. "God is in the room," he reported, paused, and added, "more than Elvis. It feels like there's a blessing on the band right now. People are saying they're feeling shivers—well, the band is as well. And I don't know what that is, but it feels like God walking through the room, and it feels like a blessing, and in the end, music is a kind of sacrament; it's not just about airplay or chart positions."

Are rock 'n' roll bands supposed to talk to *Rolling Stone* about blessings? Sacraments? God walking in the room? Why would this all sound so incredibly cliché coming from a well-scrubbed contemporary Christian rocker created by Nashville, yet actually sound sincere and authentic coming from a theatrical rock star?

Bono has the reputation as rock 'n' roll's most effective and enigmatic spiritual provocateur—rattling the souls of fans all over the globe. "I sometimes think I have a kind of Tourette's syndrome where if you're not supposed to say something, it becomes very attractive to do so," he once confessed. "You're in a rock band— what can't you talk about? God? Ok, here we go. You're supposed to write songs about sex and drugs. Well, no I won't."

Most of the world is tired of being berated and tutored about social issues by spoiled and over-paid rock stars, yet we still give an audience to Bono whose heart bleeds with the best of them. Pope John Paul II wanted to wear his sunglasses when they met. Arch-conservative senator Jesse Helms cried when he heard Bono describe the plight of hungry children in Africa. Bono has done more single-handedly to relieve Third World debt than all the Armani-clad finance ministers that could be packed into a United Nations conference room. He has a mysterious charisma, an unpretentious grace that affords him the ability to be the only one wearing sunglasses indoors without coming off as a megalomaniac. Would one dare to say he had an anointing to be a rock star?

It seems as though there is a riddle to unwrapping the significance, relevance and longevity of U2. Very little is ever predictable about their next sound. They never seem to follow rock 'n' roll's party line. They seem to be in the MTV world, but not of it. There is an underground river of depth that rolls through the tracks of U2's recordings. They make you think and invite you to imagine.

For more than twenty years, U2 has done their part to puncture the power of nihilism and hopelessness by pointing listeners to a transcendent reality of heaven, hell, angels, demons, deliverance, redemption, grace and peace. Their lyrics unfold a world beyond the things that can be merely seen and rationally grasped. The music is not a simplistic mish-mash of yummy lyrics about skipping with Jesus through fields of daisies. Instead, their songs wrestle with pain and frustration without catering to hopelessness.

In this book, Steve Stockman has been a faithful interpreter of the spiritual trek of the members of U2. There is very little garden-variety evangelicalism (in the North American sense of the word) found in the members of the band. They drink, smoke, swear and wear leather pants. But there is a hefty and poetic theological substance that I think would startle St. Paul and would bring a smile to the Psalmist. This rock 'n' roll band is committed to social justice and eternal truth. In this day and age, that is no small luxury.

For those willing to take the time to look, popular music is brimming with songs of spiritually energized quests; some worth avoiding, but many worth engaging. Artists and fans alike have seen what is on the world's buffet table and are still growling with hunger pangs. Stockman does a tremendous service to those who follow Jesus, as well as those who aren't traveling that path. To those who count themselves among the faithful, Stockman will help you open the eyes of your soul to intellectually and spiritually engage the music that touches the deepest part of what it means to be human. To those who do not consider themselves believers, this book will go a long way in helping explain why U2's music seems to scratch an unidentifiable itch.

When I saw U2 during their most recent tour, I was amazed at how often I felt the presence of God in the arena. Granted, I am a U2 fan and not a terribly objective rock critic. Nevertheless, God used the opportunity to speak to me throughout the night.

Not being a well-attuned mystic, I was rather surprised. The culmination of the evening was the final encore. After thanking "the Almighty" numerous times, Bono began singing the word *hallelujah* over and over and over again. This rather contagious melody and message rang throughout the audience's soul. Soon, it seemed as though all 16,000 fans in the arena were singing the song with Bono. This one word, *hallelujah*—praise ye the Lord. With that, they walked off the stage.

The great theologian George Eldon Ladd used to press the point that the Kingdom of God was both already and not yet; some of the ramifications of the Kingdom are realized now, while some will not be manifest until the Second Coming. As I sang the word *hallelujah* over and over with the audience, I felt as though, just for a moment, I had been caught up in the rapturous *not yet*.

As the band was just starting off many years ago, Bono wrote the following words to his father, who just recently passed away: "[God] gives us our strength and a joy that does not depend on drink or drugs. This strength will, I believe, be the quality that will take us to the top of the music business. I hope our lives will be a testament to the people who follow us, and to the music business where never before have so many lost and sorrowful people gathered in one place pretending they're having a good time. It is our ambition to make more than good music."

It seems as though that ambition continues to be fulfilled.

Steve Beard is the editor of Good News *magazine and is the founder of* thunderstruck.org.

THREE QUESTIONS FOR BONO

If I could ask Bono three questions, what would they be? I was recently asked that while speaking at the Greenbelt Arts Festival in England. The first response that came to mind was a question my friend David Dark has had ready for the moment he might find himself in a lift with Bono: "How much Flannery O'Connor have you read?" Cool. Intellectual engagement.

I also would be intrigued to know how long it took to come up with the live extravaganza that was the Zoo TV tour. I would love to be talked through its development from the initial inspiration to the opening night and the tweaking thereafter.

The main question, though, is one that has been like a dog at my heels for the last couple of years. During that time I have watched the passion with which Bono has involved himself in the Jubilee 2000 campaign to get rid of Third World debt; I have listened to the spiritual depth of the *All That You Can't Leave*

Behind album; I have seen the band reconquer the world on its
Elevation tour, ending with thanks to the Almighty and a chorus
of hallelujahs. The question: "How have you kept the vitality of
your Christian faith so vibrant in the world of rock music and in
the absence of regular Christian fellowship?" It is for me one of
the most fascinating questions of the amazing story of U2, perhaps still the biggest rock band in the world almost twenty-five
years after being formed.

Within the Christian community of which three of U2's four members were once a part, however, my question is more likely to receive
much cynicism and be bypassed by more basic questions.

"Somebody told me that the members of U2 were once
Christians. Is that true?"

"Where do you think they stand on their faith now?"

"I saw Bono dressed up as the devil. How can a Christian do
that?"

"They seem ashamed of the Gospel, and that is no way for
Christians to be! How can they be that way if they're
Christians?"

"They drink and smoke and swear. How can you believe that
they are still Christians?"

"If they say that they haven't found what they are looking for,
they cannot possibly still be believers in Christ, can they?"

No matter where I go, when people know I am a Presbyterian

minister from Ireland, once I throw in the name U2 there is a
reaction. I have found myself in heated discussions in the United
States, South Africa, The Philippines and many, many times back
home in Ireland. The axis of the discussion has more recently
moved to cyberspace. Judging by reaction to articles on my web-

> Many have been so obsessed
> with the cigar hanging out of
> Bono's mouth that they are
> missing the radical biblical
> agenda that has fired his life
> and work.
>
> THREE QUESTIONS FOR BONO
> — THREE QUESTIONS FOR BONO

site, I have what can be described as red rags to a bull dangled in
my feedback section. Are they Christians?

The vast majority of U2 interviews and reviews over the past
twenty years touch or often concentrate on the Christian faith
that is so much a part of what the band is. Their faith isn't
ridiculed. It has never been questioned, though how they keep it
with the rock lifestyle has often been a fascination. The Christian
press and Christians in general have been the doubters. There
seems to have been a keen enthusiasm to denounce the band's
Christian members as lost. There has been confusion as to what
they have tried to do in the nineties and condemnation on their
lifestyles, which include smoking cigars, drinking Jack Daniels
and using language that is not common currency at Southern

Baptist conventions. The Christian community seems to have confined its definitions of faith to various precise behavioral patterns and clichéd statements of faith. In getting caught up in the minutia of behavioral codes that have had more to do with respectable middle-class behavior than biblical guidelines, many have been so obsessed with the cigar hanging out of Bono's

> **"U2 inhabits that dangerous and exhilarating space that connects spiritual and physical, mortal and divine."**
>
> THREE QUESTIONS FOR BONO

mouth that they are missing the radical biblical agenda that has fired his life and work.

That the band members have distanced themselves from the Church for various reasons over the years has, of course, added fuel to the fire for doubters. That the band has been adamant in not speaking to the Christian press has not helped. But in the very early days when the band did speak to Christian magazines, they were often misquoted and felt used and abused. The evangelical Christian world seemed to claim U2 as its property, and therefore, U2's members found their faith defined and explained by magazines rather than by the members themselves. Aligning themselves with the Christian press would have pigeonholed

WALK ON

01

their faith and their art, squeezed them into the mold of other peoples' expectations, and narrowed the focus of the band's influence and scope. In their work, however—whether on records, on stage, on video or in interviews—they have never denied their faith, even if at times they have questioned how that faith fits with the events of their generation. They have constantly kept spiritual issues at the heart of all they have done, whether looking at the light or the darkness around them.

U2 inhabits that dangerous and exhilarating space that connects spiritual and physical, mortal and divine. The band's music stretches every sinew of our imaginations in a most courageous attempt to take us as far as a rock 'n' roll band can. The members of U2 have filled every millimeter of the gap with the most profound social commentaries, exposing the nonsense of post-modern life. Inside and outside the lines of their art, they have campaigned for a spiritual Kingdom that they believe in but still haven't found.

Bruce Springsteen once wrote that he learned more from a three-minute record than he ever learned in school. U2 has been my lecture hall of learning for twenty years. These guys have lifted my spirit to dance on higher plains, taught me about American injustice in Central America and apartheid in South Africa, and personified how faith and the world continually caress and collide. They have led me into an understanding of what the post-modern technological world looks like and the shallow and fickle nature of the madness in which we live. A madness that is no more frenetic or bright or loud than the Zoo TV or Popmart tours.

This book is not a new exposé of U2 or a comprehensive biography of the members' lives. It is a spiritual companion to their career. It is an attempt at telling the story of the band members' journeys of faith and exposing the underlying spiritual themes in U2's music. In examining these issues, it is also essential to take a look at evangelical Christianity—the stream of faith that has both under-girded the band's work and caused them to react in anger and disillusionment when people of faith have seemed more concerned with appearances than with just responses to human suffering.

It is impossible to understand U2's perspectives toward the world, especially in the band's early work, without also understanding the unique political, religious and social climate of Northern Ireland in the late seventies and early eighties. It was a country torn by civil unrest and barbaric inhumanity in the name of God and country. The country's troubles have had a significant impact on U2 over the years because they hit close to home: Northern Ireland is located only 70 miles from the band members' boyhood homes in Dublin.

To fully understand someone, you must first understand where they come from. Aside from the restlessness of Northern Ireland, you must also understand the makeup the band's homeland in the Republic. You must understand the spiritual and musical climate of Dublin. It is an unlikely setting for this story, but probably the only one that could give birth to one of the greatest rock bands the world would ever know.

02

DUBLIN CITY, IRELAND

Dublin City, Ireland, might have been the last place that such a thing would be expected to happen, but it was conceivably the only place in the English-speaking western world that the U2 phenomenon of conundrum could have been minted. Some people joke that if you ask an Irishman for directions, he might be quick to answer, "Well if I were going there, I would not start here." At the end of the seventies, if you wanted to audition for the job of biggest rock band on the planet, you would not have started in music-starved Dublin.

Yet when *Hot Press* journalist Bill Graham began championing U2 seventeen months before it released its first single, there was something about the band that suggested, or near prophesied, that they were destined to go places. Even in that first article, while the band members were still at school, Graham used words such as "contenders," "professional" and "vocation." The band members, too, had an almost arrogant belief in their destiny. In their first mention in *Rolling Stone* magazine in February 1981, lead singer Bono said, "I don't mean to sound arrogant, but at this stage, I do feel we were meant to be one of the great groups. There's a certain spark, a certain chemistry, that was special about the Stones, The Who, The Beatles and I think is also special about U2." [1]

Ten years later, in 1991, Dublin had become one of the coolest cities in Europe and was chosen the European City of Culture. As a result of a government scheme encouraging the rich and famous to spend their money there and granting tax-exemption to artists, many rock stars were happy to make it their home. Dublin was dubbed the city of 1,000 bands. On every street corner, somebody was trying to make it in the music business. The Hot House Flowers, Emotional Fish, Fat Lady Sings and Engine Alley were just a few of the bands signed to major international deals as the city on the banks of the Liffey became what Liverpool had been in the early sixties. Of course, few of these bands broke out from their parochial popularity, but at the beginning of the third millennium you will find Irish acts dominating UK music charts. Names like Ronan Keating and his old band Boyzone, Westlife and Bewitched have the teen market sown up. And, of course, The Corrs, The Cranberries and the infamous Sinead O'Connor have achieved worldwide success.

U2 was not the result of such a healthy music scene. It was the cause of it. When CBS released U2's first vinyl record, an EP titled "U2-3" in Ireland in September 1979, there was little happening in the way of Irish rock. In the Republic, Rory Gallagher and Thin Lizzy had reached beyond the shores but could hardly have been said to be on a world stage. The year earlier, The

Boomtown Rats' song "Rat Trap" reached number one on UK single charts—the first Irish band to achieve this. The Rats' break-

> ## U2 was not the result of such a healthy music scene. It was the cause of it.

DUBLIN CITY, IRELAND

through raised the hopes of Dublin bands, but to have ideas of grandeur was still to fantasize against the odds rather than be an inheritor of any kind of birthright.

Yet Dublin's punk scene was burgeoning, giving many young wanna-bes the energy to make noise and dream big. And though it never could have been labeled as such, U2 arrived on the slip-stream of new wave adrenaline. Through the band's passionate live shows and the charismatic antics of its front man, the band got noticed. Their manager, Paul McGuinness, discovered them playing The Project and later said it was not their competence, but their raw energy that drew him. By the time their debut album, *Boy*, was released in October 1980, there was no limit to people's predictions for the group.

The reason? *Boy* shone with originality. Producer Steve Lillywhite had harnessed the promise of the band's early singles. Everything

WALK ON

02

was built around a ringing guitar sound that The Edge conjured
through a cheap Memory Man echo unit that Bono had bought
him. It was with that sound that they began to build an album
and, some would say, a career. *Boy* was vibrant, passionate, lively.
It had a sense of searching restlessness that would best describe
the adolescence that the lyrics attempted to tackle and would be
a trait that followed these guys into manhood.

Bono said the album's song "Twilight" was "about the grey area
of adolescence, that twilight zone where the boy that was con-
fronts the man to be in the shadows. It is about the confusion,
pain and occasional exhilaration that results from that confrontation." [2] If ever a guitarist could take that sentiment and put
it through an amplifier, it was The Edge. That's what *Boy* is all about.

When it comes to songwriting, Bono would admit that he didn't
discover the art until the group's 1987 release, *The Joshua Tree*.
But in U2's early albums, he was able to reach deep within himself and find lyrics that expressed what his peers were feeling. It
was his honesty more than his literary ability that made *Boy* so
endearing. Whether it was dealing with suicide on "A Day
Without Me" and seeing his own ego being surrendered (a recurring theme for U2), or youthful dreaming of stardom and changing the world in "The Ocean," or confronting his mother's death
on "I Will Follow," a young man was dealing with his world eye
to eye. Looking at life in the eye would become a trademark of
Bono's lyric-writing.

At the time, U2 would always dismiss the band's punk influence.
At their early gigs, they would make it a point to cover songs by
the likes of Peter Frampton, The Rolling Stones and even The Bay

WALK ON

02

City Rollers—and nothing by The Undertones, Stiff Little Fingers or The Sex Pistols. It would be more than twenty years before U2 would turn to the punk catalog, when in 2000 the band name-checked the New York scene of the late seventies and played "I Remember You" by The Ramones at The Irving Plaza in New York City. Joey Ramone passed away a few months later during the first leg of the Elevation tour, and there would be much eulogizing. The Edge told the *Chicago Tribune*: "We didn't sound like The Ramones, but what we got from The Ramones was more fundamental and central: They were the reason we became a band. Having seen The Ramones play, and then The Clash soon after, it was like, 'Whoa! We can be part of this. These guys have done it their way, and we will find our way.' There was sense that the door of possibility had swung wide open." [3]

Punk may have been the musical motivation behind *Boy*, but there was another significant dimension to the band members' work—their Christian faith. During Bill Graham's first full-length interview with Bono, he stunned Graham by announcing abruptly, "One other thing you should know…we're all Christians." [4] U2's bass player, Adam, was not a Christian, but he was an exception to the rule in that group. Graham expressed concern about this revelation in his book *Another Time, Another Place*: "I, a typically Irish ex-Catholic agnostic, feared for their reputation. Born-again Christianity could hinder their career—a view which, the more I pondered it, was riven with illogicalities." [5] Those fears were well-founded, but had the band been from anywhere but Dublin there would have been less chance of overcoming such hindrances.

Many other young Christians have tried to make it in the world

WALK ON

of rock music and failed for many reasons. But it is not necessarily the worldview of Christianity that is the obstacle so much as it is the isolated subculture that the Church has created. Dublin was a city where U2's new, young, zealous believers were not going to get drawn into any Church subculture.

"One other thing you should know...we're all Christians."

DUBLIN CITY, IRELAND

Since its start, U2 has lived its art in the eye of a storm that has been kicking up dust since the days Jesus walked the streets of earth. In Jesus' day, the Pharisees strictly differentiated between what was sacred and what was profane. Today in the United States and Northern Ireland—two places of particular reference to U2—there is a similar dualism at work, and it has put bands like U2 under pressure regarding where they perform and what they say.

If U2 had been in fellowship in the United States or even just sixty miles north of Dublin, in Northern Ireland, it would have been easy to get sucked into a Christian subculture. Many bands in similar situations are discouraged from playing in secular venues like bars or clubs because Christians shouldn't be in these places. The theory is that you shouldn't take Jesus into what are often called "dens of iniquity." The only acceptable reason for attending these places would be to evangelize the lost who go there.

As a result of this mindset, many talented musicians are steered into a gospel band scenario, going from church to church singing cliché-driven songs with limited content. The audience members are almost exclusively Christian, and, as the majority of them already have assented to the beliefs being preached from the stage, the clichés are wasted. A safe Christian industry ghetto is created with pop stars and record companies. There is a magazine, *Contemporary Christian Music*, which has become the label for the entire industry—an industry that is always in danger of ending up culturally irrelevant. When Jesus told His disciples they were the light of the world, where did He want them to shine? (Matt. 5:14) As more beams of light that make the light shine blindingly bright upon itself, or as strobes of illumination flashing radical alternative lifestyles across the darkness? Do you blame the dark for being dark, or the light for not shining?

In the early eighties, Os Guinness, one of the most intellectual Christian writers of our time, wrote a book titled *Gravedigger File*. Based on C.S. Lewis' *The Screwtape Letters*, a book that would sneak its way into the U2 story, it was written from the viewpoint of a senior devil outlining the strategy of subverting the Church from within. One of the most powerful schemes for doing this would be to make Christianity "privately engaging but socially irrelevant." [6] Christians can have all the energy and resources that the Church can muster, which can be enormous, but if they spend all their time looking in at themselves rather than looking out, the devil will be pleased. It's why Christian singer Rich Mullins signed all his autographs "Be God's." He was aware that people could "be good" and still make the devil smile with their ineffectualness.

UK's Delirious? is an example of a band that has suffered from the constraints of the Christian industry ghetto. Emerging out of a community church scene on the south coast of England, Delirious? has been trying to crack the UK mainstream for years. Originally experimenting in their local youth group, the members of Delirious? discovered a worship sound that drew a following far beyond that group. Soon they began filling major venues across Britain and entered the UK Top 20 with "Deeper," as radio-friendly a pop rock tune as any.

However, even though their future single "See a Star" reached number sixteen and their *Mezzamorphis* album reached number thirteen, they seem to have been shunned by *Top of the Pops*, Radio 1 and the other major media support that could propel them into the higher plains of rock stardom and influence. There could be various reasons for the stumbling block. Their first album that attempted to break new ground, *King of Fools*, might have had too many references rooted in the ghetto, dealing with spiritual issues that critics and secular music fans might not have been able to understand. Maybe they had a rabid little bunch of paranoid fans who believed their favorites were being prejudiced against because of their faith and made nuisances of themselves to editors and programmers. Or maybe those fans were right; maybe it is easier to be accepted in the mainstream if you are Buddhist or Muslim than if you are followers of Jesus.

Whatever the reason, U2 did not face such difficulties because in Dublin there was no such Christian ghetto and, therefore, no such exclusively Christian fan base. They were not in any need to break out of one thing to crack the other.

The Republic of Ireland is ninety-six percent Roman Catholic, and the evangelical subculture is predominantly Protestant. The fact that U2, looking at the members' parents, was five-eighths Protestant is a phenomenon in itself, but that they formed a band and discovered a fervent evangelicalism at the same time without getting caught up in some kind of dualism was only possible because of their location. With Irish evangelicals so small in number, integration of faith and daily living is vital. There are no Christian venues for budding Christians trying to do something in rock. If you do not make it in the real world, you do not make it.

So while the three teenage Christian members of U2—Bono, The Edge and Larry—were immersing themselves in Bible studies and beginning to make efforts to create an impression in the local music scene, Bono and The Edge were also running around with a motley group of eccentric, young, wild boys called Lypton Village. It was the Village that gave Bono and The Edge their names. The other band in the musical fraternity, The Virgin Prunes, wore eye makeup and dresses and had a wild perform-ance art-type set. Some of these guys, too, were passionate about a newfound Christian faith, and in these early days, there seems to have been no contradictions in that.

At the earliest point in U2's formative years, spirituality and music were allowed to run together. Few bands with three such impassioned and fervent new believers would have had the free-dom from within and without to record an album like *Boy* on

their time off from Bible studies. *Boy* is about adolescence and the benefits of being unshackled by missionary expectations, which would try to weigh them down without success, as they pushed out from Dublin to conquer the world.

On *Boy*, "I Will Follow" is the song that perhaps best touches on the faith within the band. Bono sings, "*I was lost, I am found.*" As he would do seventeen years later on "Mofo" from the group's Pop album, Bono was interweaving the loss of his mother and finding God. "I Will Follow" would be their most enduring song. This was a song about adolescent tragedy as well as discipleship, skillfully disguised but just as powerful. This type of skillful disguise would become another trademark of U2's work.

In Howard Sounes' biography of Bob Dylan, *Down the Highway*, band member T-Bone Burnett spoke of Dylan's conversion to Christ: "Beginning in 1976, something happened all across the world. It happened to Bono and The Edge and Larry Mullens (of U2) in Ireland. It happened to Michael Hutchence (of INXS) in Australia, and it happened here in Los Angeles: There was spiritual movement." [7] Burnett himself was converted to Christianity, along with fellow band members Steven Soles and David Mansfield on Bob Dylan's Rolling Thunder Review tour. INXS did play the Australian Christian circuit for a little time, though how spiritual their reasons for doing so is a little blurred. Dylan himself would confess faith in Christ, too. There is little doubt that something unique and out of the blue was happening in Dublin. Bono was the first to find God, and it seems he was the one who led the others into charismatic and evangelical Christianity by way of the Shalom fellowship.

Bono had a few encounters with Christianity. As a child, he regularly visited his neighbors, the Rowans. Robbie Rowan was a member of the Brethren. His son Derek, nicknamed Guggi, was one of Bono's early accomplices. Guggi later became one of The Virgin Prunes, along with Bono's soul brother, Gavin Friday. Trevor "Strongman" Rowan was also a Prune, and his younger brother Peter was later the cover face of *Boy* and *War*. Bono would go to Bible studies and revival meetings with the Rowans and attend a Boys Club at the YMCA.

If what was happening on his street nudged Bono God-ward, what was happening in his school gave him a shove. Mount Temple was a liberally minded seat of learning that was experimental in being the first non-denominational school in a country that was still in the grips of the Roman Catholic Church. The school attracted progressive and creative teachers, most of whom had a more open view of Church things and some of whom had a free and serious commitment to Christian faith. One such teacher was Sophie Shirley, whom Bono once described as someone who "really showed us what God can do in someone's life, and although we fought against her and threw bricks at her and stoned her in the name of adolescent freedom, we all inwardly respected her, and she had a deep effect on us." [8]

In the late seventies, something spectacular was happening in Mount Temple. The school had just changed its name and ethos from the traditional gown-wearing Rugby school Mountjoy and Marine to this new progressive experiment. Change was in the air. Prayer meetings were taking place every morning, and at lunchtime, upwards of one hundred students would meet for praise. There were barbecues on the beach at Rush, north county

WALK ON

Dublin, at which Bono was known to do a campfire version of
the popular Christian chorus "Light Up the Fire." Many of the
prefects were Christians, and the prefects' room became another
location for God chat and fellowship. Everywhere you turned it
seemed people were becoming Christians.

A respected teacher at the school, Jack Heaslip, offered support
and sympathy to Bono. Being a believer in Christ in any way
other than having been baptized and confirmed and going to
Mass once a week would have been a bit weird in late seventies
Dublin. Heaslip seemed to have great empathy with Bono and
would be an encouragement to the spiritual happenings at that
time. Heaslip later became a Church of Ireland minister and performed the marriage ceremony of Bono and his childhood
sweetheart, Alison Stewart, whom he met at Mount Temple in
1982. Bono continues to thank him on album sleeves, and he
continued to go on the road with the band even to the start of its
2001 Elevation tour.

Don Moxham, a history teacher at the school who also developed relationships with his students, struck up a friendship with
the boys in U2. They had many long "talk sessions." Moxham
believed teaching was as important in the informal interconnec-
tions as in the classroom. Moxham was a positive influence on
his students—especially these fledgling musicians. He was no charismatic, but he had a deep faith and would touch U2 for years to
come. Musically, Albert Bradshaw, like Moxham, went beyond his
duties to inspire especially The Edge to develop his love of music,
technical ability, and exploration of melodies and chords.

Bill Graham suggests that the spiritually liberal Mount Temple reinforced U2's faith in God. He suggests that had the guys gone to a traditional Catholic school instead, they would have turned to the anti-Catholic agnostic ways of himself, their manager, Paul McGuinness, or Boomtown Rats' Bob Geldof.

> For many years the band members said that their faith—not their rock 'n' roll lifestyle—was the real rebellion.
>
> DUBLIN CITY, IRELAND

One incident led to a few of the U2 members becoming Christians, according to The Edge. While some in their teenage gang, Lypton Village, were in McDonald's one afternoon, a Hare Krishna began abusing a man who was reading the Bible. When the boys joined the man, Denis Sheedy, partly out of curiosity and maybe to support him, they struck up a friendship. It was because of this that they started to attend the Shalom community.

Bono had been searching in that direction for a while before Larry and The Edge. Soon after meeting Sheedy, they were going to Bible studies and prayer group gatherings. The Edge said: "There was sort of a move in Dublin in those early days. Bono was the only real Christian then. He started sharing his feelings and thoughts about God. And it seemed a natural progression from what was happening in school to go along to the meetings

WALK ON

02

outside school. I realized that that was where it was at, and about the same time, Larry and I became Christians." [9]

Writer John Waters asked Bono in 1993 if he had always been a believer. Bono replied, "No. I knew." He explained the great attraction that liberating faith was to him. "I suppose it's the idea," Bono replied. "Judeo Christianity is about the idea that God is interested in you—as opposed to a god is interested in you. This was a radical thought: that God who created the universe might be interested in me...It is the most extraordinary thought." [10]

The idea of it being radical attracted U2. In any other city in the western world, this kind of Christian behavior would have been seen as old-fashioned and almost nerdish. In any other city, Bono would have laughed at such middle class, respectable, religious behavior. But in Dublin, this was radical stuff. To take Jesus seriously was far out. In some ways, Shalom was an out-there kind of gang on parallel lines with the Lypton Village gang. It wasn't as if one of them was dangerous and the other one safe.

For many years the band members said that their faith—not their rock 'n' roll lifestyle—was the real rebellion. In 1983, Bono told *Rolling Stone*: "I think that, ultimately, the group is totally rebellious because of our stance against what people accept as rebellion. The whole thing about rock stars driving cars into swimming pools—that's not rebellion...Rebellion starts at home, in your heart, in your refusal to compromise your beliefs and your values. I'm not interested in politics like people fighting back with sticks and stones, but in the politics of love." [11] For this band, it was more rebellious to be reading Bibles in the back of the tour bus than it was to be doing drugs—a perspective on

Christianity that was not a cultural norm. But being from a place where those with intense spiritual faith were the minority helped the band members grab hold of the radical edge of following Jesus.

Over the last twenty years, U2's music and discussion of its own Christian freedoms have made an impression on the spiritual landscape of modern Dublin. There have been huge changes in how young Dubliners look at God and faith. In what is a traditionally Roman Catholic country, young people have increasingly voiced a strong belief in Jesus even though they rarely go to Mass. Belief has become much more personal and not restricted to the voice of traditional church hierarchy.

The guys in U2 have made their faith in Jesus Christ known. They have made it clear that though they had feet in both camps of Ireland's denominational divide, they found a personal relationship with God outside of both. For two decades, U2 has seemed suspicious of any organized religion. The band members have believed their faith lived and thrived outside the narrow gates of religion. Bono once said, "I have this hunger in me...everywhere I look, I see the evidence of a Creator. But I don't see it as religion, which has cut my people in two. I don't see Jesus Christ as being any part of a religion. Religion to me is almost like when God leaves—and people devise a set of rules to fill the space." [12]

OCTOBER

U2's second album, *October*, landed on critics' desks "with a shout"—as one of its songs is titled—in August, 1981. The shout was a cry of strong spiritual confession; so strong, in fact, Neil McCormick's review in *Hot Press* called *October* "a Christian LP." [1] With titles like "Gloria" and "Rejoice" and mentions of the cross in "Tomorrow" and "With a Shout (Jerusalem)," the songs dig deep with a passionate searching and reach out to the heavens in a way that is highly intoxicating. Rarely has Christianity collided with rock music in such force or with such rich reward. *October* was the first declaration to the outside world of the spiritual twist in the U2 story.

U2 had been garnering a rabid little following from its extensive live gigging, but *Boy* had not exactly broken any sales records. This second album surely would have to capture the kind of response their charismatic performances were receiving. Could the spiritual preoccupations of *October* be accepted? The unveiling of these new Christian anthems came when U2 was the supporting act to Thin Lizzy in a concert at Slane Castle, on the banks of the Boyne River north of Dublin. The band members hurled themselves into their set, singing about Jerusalem and "*a cross on the side of a hill, where blood was spilled.*" It was bold and zealous. There was uncertainty in the crowd—perhaps more than new material typically draws. But by the time they got to "Gloria" and "Rejoice," the audience seemed to get past the band's evangelical zeal. They seemed to realize that even though they were not sure about this subject matter, they were going to get on board the great ride of celebratory rock music that made this band the most exciting around.

It could not have been seen as a cunning plan or a shrewd marketing ploy to bring such a Christian-focused album into a rock world that was usually dismissive of such things. There were few artists who had ever been able to effectively hold their Christian faith before a rock music audience. Cliff Richard, Britain's equivalent of Elvis Presley, cashed in his rebellious sneering lip for a laughed-at, respectable smile when he went public about his conversion in the mid-sixties. Bob Dylan won a Grammy Award for the song "Gonna Serve Somebody" from his Christian album, *Slow Train Coming*, two years earlier, but his more recent albums *Saved* and *Shot of Love* did not met with a sympathetic press. Many saw it as a nail in the coffin of his career.

Hot Press, the Irish music paper that has followed U2's career through journalists Bill Graham, Niall Stokes, Neil McCormick and Joe Jackson, has defined the band's history. *Hot Press* discovered U2 and was the champion of the cause, even though it has not given much good press to anything related to Christianity.

The paper constantly takes cheap swipes at the Roman Catholic Church, the predominant religion in the Republic of Ireland. The scandals within that religion and its conservative approach to birth control, abortion, divorce, etc., have made it an antithesis of the progressive rock culture that has developed in Ireland in the *Hot Press* years. That this paper took the crusading Christian U2 to its heart is an exception to its rule.

The exuberance and vitality of the sound U2 cast across Dublin was enough to see the band through any misunderstandings of its faith-infused music. That the band was local and seemed destined for megastardom may have helped. That U2 had been discovered by the fledgling music paper perhaps gave the band a whole lot of grace. That the band's school friend Neil McCormick reviewed it may have added to the sympathetic coverage of *October*. But whatever the reasons, the music press chose to deal with the incongruity of the band's blatant faith on a quality rock album rather than simply dismissing it. It might be a lesson to Christians who feel the music press is prejudiced against them: If you make great music, the content will not hinder it.

Behind the scenes, the band members themselves were trying to come to terms with whether they would deal with it or dismiss it. Bono, Larry and The Edge had become more involved in the Shalom fellowship. They were just twenty years old and had discovered their faith amid an enflamed charismatic revival. Questions of ego and fame and the seemingly trivial pursuit of rock music were beginning to arise. There seemed to be a wind of change within the Shalom community and its leadership. Remember, the Lypton Villagers had lived parallel to and relatively comfortably with Shalom. But somewhere along the way,

WALK ON

03

there was a closing in of behavioral patterns. It may have been that the great evangelical movement on the cusp of which the Villagers joined the fellowship was more sympathetic to their weaknesses and quirks in order to draw them in. Once involved, when things again returned to normal and regular fellowship numbers, then the legalists began to turn the screw.

While the band was on tour between *Boy* and the recording of *October*, a member of the north Dublin satellite of the community claimed to have a prophecy that God wanted the band to give up. When the band members returned to the fellowship, which at that time they craved and thrived upon, they were looking forward to the support of their spiritual family. Instead, they entered a tense situation where the fellowship was split over whether God wanted U2 to carry on or pack up their instruments.

In his book *Far Away So Close* about the exploits around the Zoo TV tour, B.P. Fallon recalls a morning when after recording and without a key to his own hotel room in Dublin, Bono, Gavin Friday and he had a fry up in a café off Capel Street. Upon their return to Bono's car, the singer shows them a place where, he said, "I used to go to revival meetings there...the place would be on fire! Studying the Bible, that kind of stuff. I miss it..." [2] Given that Bono, The Edge and Larry were young kids caught up in such a fire, it is little wonder that their souls were in turmoil as they attempted to untangle their future. The miracle is probably that they came out of it and decided to go on. The pressure could have easily deafened out the music. They saw it as a pull between the world and the Lord, but it seems that it may have been a pull between the devil and the deep blue sea. The question of the usefulness of rock music and art in general has been a huge debate within Christendom for some time. If The Edge, Bono and Larry had been coming under the influence of such preaching, it would be understandable that when the same young exuberance that was rocking the world at that time was channeled into thinking about Christ, there would be an intense focus on the dilemma.

> Questions of ego and fame and the seemingly trivial pursuit of rock music were beginning to arise.

OCTOBER

This is where the downside of their isolation kicked in. Though the lack of Christian industry ghetto in Dublin helped them from having their art curtailed, it hurt when they needed advice from other Christians in the arts. They made an unannounced appearance at the Greenbelt Arts Festival in England in August 1981. Greenbelt has long been the biggest Christian arts festival in Europe and has been a pioneer in encouraging Christians to take their art out of the ghetto. The band made some lifelong connections at Greenbelt, and the event, though Bono would only make one more appearance there as a steward, would ease their sense of spiritual loneliness.

Andy McCarroll, the top Christian singer in Belfast, was someone whom the band respected and listened to at the time. He had made two Dylan-inspired solo albums in the late seventies before becoming excited by new-wave and forming Moral Support. With some of the rawness left over from punk and McCarroll's snarling voice, the group performed some intelligent Christian songs. It seems The Edge was especially taken with McCarroll's magnetic stage presence, natural songwriting ability and the spiritual intensity of the production. The Edge would eventually invite McCarroll to Dublin for a weekend just to shoot the breeze about the purpose of what they were trying to achieve.

In a twist, McCarroll's spiritual support base decided that Moral Support should come off the road in early 1982. The group's first album, *Zionic Bonds*, had sold well. The band was filling any venue in Northern Ireland. The members had been high up the bill at the Greenbelt that U2 attended and were on the verge of opening up all kinds of possibilities worldwide. Then there was a change in attitude with the leadership of their fellowship. In Ireland in the early eighties, there were many fellowship groups like Shalom that had started outside of any accountability of established churches. One of the trends was to set in place pastoral care that became much too strict and controlling. The pastor told people what decisions to make in their everyday lives. Some even had a shepherding system where everyone was designated someone to whom to be accountable.

The leaders in Moral Support's Belfast fellowship felt, maybe as a result of difficulties, that the band was not able to cope spiritually with the life of a rock band on the road. Like a car needing an overhaul, the band was asked "to come off the road for a time" until everything was put right. There was an errant but fashionable Christian virtue then that suggested that "laying it down for the Lord," especially while so successful, would be the righteous thing to do. The fame and the danger of getting caught up in the adulation could lead to compromise. There was also a strange slant on discipleship, which called people to surrender what they were good at or enjoyed. McCarroll was a gifted songwriter with a natural flare for pop melodies and a gripping live presence. He didn't perform another song for more than a decade, and in the end, had personal and spiritual crises that may be attributed to a church's decision to take him away from his vocation. The same thing happened to another charismatic Belfast performer, Brian Houston, a few years later. Houston, however, after a few years of frustration and dissatisfaction with his post-musical life, went against his church leader's advice and returned to the stage, pioneered a booming Belfast club scene as well as later becoming an internationally known worship leader. U2 would have lived with that kind of news and peer pressure filtering through the Irish charismatic fellowships.

It would be wrong to suggest that these are not serious issues that need to be dealt with. To be a Christian and to find that you are a gifted musician with a contemporary slant brings with it certain questions and responsibilities. It is a field fraught with temptations in drugs and sex and materialism, and it is an easy place to lose your head with the intoxication of fame or even lose your very soul in trying to gain the world. It is the place where the members of U2 found themselves around the time of *October*.

Jesus told a parable about a master who gave his servants money and went off to another country (Matt. 25:14-30). On his return he asked the servants what they had done with the money. Some had put it to work to make more money, but one servant simply gave it back to the master saying that he simply kept it safe. The master was angry with that servant. The lesson from the parable is that when you are given a gift, you have to use it. You have to deal with the responsibility and dilemmas of it. You cannot run from it. You cannot hide your light under some bushel of safety and hope that it just goes away. You've got to face the consequences of who you are and what your vocation is.

In 1981, U2 could have given in to someone's prophecy that was based on good intentions of trying to give good Christian advice. But where would they be now? What would it have done to their spirits and their souls to be taken away from this avenue of creativity that obviously burned within them? Who might have they become? For sure, the rock world would have missed one of the most influential bands of the latter part of the twentieth century. Imagine a world without *The Joshua Tree* and *Achtung Baby*. Imagine no Zoo TV or Popmart tour. Imagine the biblical imagery and spiritual provocation that would have been absent from the world's record stores, pop charts, MTV programming and music press.

October was recorded in the dilemma of deliberation over these issues. The Edge would later tell Bill Flanagan: "*October* was a struggle from beginning to end. It was an incredibly hard record for us to make because we had major problems at the time. And I had been through this thing of really not knowing if I should be in the band or not...It was reconciling two things that seemed for us to be mutually exclusive. We never did resolve the contradiction. That's the truth. And probably never will." [3]

There was another problem that the three band members' faith had brought. There was a danger at this time of division within their very ranks. Adam was into the whole rock 'n' roll lifestyle, and even though the others were Christians they still had great chemistry at making vibrant rock 'n' roll. But during the recording of *October* something changed. There was a new soapbox fervor in the proselytizing lyrics, maybe even written to appease the doubters in the fellowship. The recording sessions of *October* were peppered with praise and prayer times, as the band's friends who shared their faith and their belief that they were doing God's will by keeping at the music came to support them in seeking God's blessing on the songs. Windmill Lane was constantly switching roles from being a church to being a recording studio. Adam was aware of all that had been going on around Mount Temple and seemed to accept not only that it was part of who the guys were, but also that whatever this Christian thing was, it added something special to the band. Still, he and Paul McGuinness felt out in the cold as Bible studies took place on the tour bus and other places. Time resolved this uneasiness, and Bono asking Adam, not The Edge, Larry or another member of Shalom, to be his best man in 1982 was a huge gesture of acceptance.

This feeling of acceptance continued twenty years later. In 2001, Adam was not necessarily comfortable with the way the band's spirituality was portrayed, but he admitted that something special happens at U2 gigs: "I don't know what it is…but I definitely know when it's there. It doesn't happen every night, but some nights, there's a sense of community and fellowship. And people have said there's a spiritual aspect to what's happening in the house." [4] The one in the band who has never made any public confession of a Christian faith or ever spoken on things spiritual seems to have come to terms with that vital part of the band's makeup. Likewise, during interviews for John Waters' book *Race of Angels*, The Edge recognizes that Adam's presence in the band was a positive friction to its early zealous spiritual focus. [5] Having a skeptic so close to their sense of vocation forced the

> "The central faith and spirit of the band is the same. But I have less and less time for legalism now. I just see that you live a life of faith."
>
> — OCTOBER

band members to apply their faith to wider issues than if they had been a naive, homogeneous bunch of believers.

Besides the spiritual upheaval and uncertainty, the band encountered another problem during the days of *October*. Bono had all of his lyrics stolen on the U.S. tour prior to recording. When it came time to hit the studio, the guys were running short of time and Bono was struggling on every front. Considering these circumstances, *October* was a powerful piece of work. The best word to describe it may be celebration. It was uplifting and joyful. It was worship music like no one had ever attempted to achieve— maybe because it hadn't been written as such. "Gloria" is nothing short of a thumping rock hymn. "Tomorrow," again showing

Bono's penchant for weaving his mother and God into the same song, has you looking to the skies in expectation that they would rip in two and the Messiah would return to change the whole world order. "Rejoice" and "Scarlet," which simply repeated *rejoice*, were reclaiming words that had been lost as archaic in the minds of most young people.

Besides the bombastic rejoicing and the looking up to see God, the album also had the honest soul searching that was the mark of *Boy*. There was still the need to throw bricks through windows. Hints of the questioning about what they should be doing also were audible. In "Gloria," Bono tells God, "*Oh Lord, if I had anything, anything at all, I'd give it to you.*" Would that mean giving up the music? In the same song, he realizes it is not in fame or music, but "*only in You I'm complete.*" That reflection that he is keen to throw a brick through is realizing that he is "*going nowhere,*" which wasn't exactly a description of their career potential then. Was there another way? Was the music meaningless? On "With a Shout," that omnipresent question starts the song, "*Oh where do we go/ Where do we go from here/ Where'd we go?*" The album ends with a limp and trivial lyric, unless you are writing from such a cauldron of confusion. Bono goes on about singing songs and ends with, "*Is that all you want from me?*" Is there more, or is that indeed what these guys were created for?

Bono would say a few years later, "Yeah, we were a bit uptight at one stage, though you must remember that with Lypton Village and so on, we weren't coming from an at all pious or monk-like existence. But at the same time when we first started exploring the teachings of Christ and studying the Scriptures, we got involved in something that on one level was opening our minds to a wider reality but which on another just closed us off to certain experiences. But you know you go through things." [6] The Edge would say something similar: "I suppose we've changed our attitudes a lot since then. The central faith and spirit of the band is the same. But I have less and less time for legalism now. I just see that you live a life of faith." [7]

Somehow, as Bono says, they got through it. How close it was, only the band knew. What saved them from it, maybe only God knows. Perhaps Gavin Friday and Guggi becoming a little suspicious of the Shalom goings on sent alarm bells to their fellow Lypton Villagers. The two Virgin Prunes had left the fellowship for various reasons, and maybe the band members were more committed to their fellow Villagers than to Shalom. Certainly the fact that the fellowship was only one of the voices of peer pressure, influence and accountability was a blessing. Guggi and Friday are still in-house confidants of U2's life and art to this day. Even in the interviews that followed the release of *All That You Can't Leave Behind* in 2000, Bono would say of them: "We've released experimental records, or whatever, but we've never released a crap record. That's because we have people around us. The band first of all. And then people like Gavin and Guggi." [8]

In living ever since in the contradiction that The Edge says they have never resolved, the members of U2 have lived on the edge of a cliff dividing the sacred and the profane. No one would say they have lived on that thin line between heaven and hell without at times dipping their feet into the fires and getting burned in the process. But surely they have lived out the balances in as successful a way as most other Christians in the arts. They have dealt with it better than the ghetto called Christian music.

At a recent Christian youth leaders conference in the United States, Steve Taylor, founder of Squint Entertainment (label of crossover hit Sixpence None the Richer) and a successful crossover Christian artist in his own right, spoke to thousands of youth leaders about how Christian artists could best serve God. He showed with simple logic how the music industry was the most influential factor on the development of young people and that as a Christian, he felt this influence was not good. It was far from it. He then made it clear that the problem lay with the Church: "You reap what you sow, and we have reaped nothing because we have sown nothing in that world" [9] (2 Cor. 9:6). Taylor touched on an issue that the Christians in U2 must have been dealing with during the days they spent wondering where to turn. The Christian Church has put a spiritual hierarchy on jobs. Ministers and missionaries are on top, then perhaps doctors and nurses come next, and so on to the bottom, where artists appear. Artists of whatever kind have to compromise everything to entertain. Art is fluffy froth that is no good in the Kingdom of God. What nonsense. The place Christians need to be to make an impact is at the forefront of the music industry, where the most influence is exerted.

U2 has shown the way. These guys have made mistakes along the way, but maybe the Church should take some of the blame. As Taylor says, "You reap what you sow," and the Church has been slow to support the life and art of U2. Maybe the times they have stumbled and admitted their imperfections have been worth the risk to be boundary-pushers in a world the Church has neglected. Jesus always seemed happier with followers who would chop people's ears off with swords (Matt. 26:51) than He was with people who claimed to have kept all the commandments.

WALK ON

"SUNDAY BLOODY SUNDAY"

Bono interrupted the euphoria of U2's pre-Christmas Maysfield Hall gig in Belfast. It was December, 1982, and the band's third album, *War*, was slated to release the following March. The three-thousand-person, sell-out crowd was enraptured by Bono climbing on top of anything he could, giving every ounce of his being to that which he was made for. But in the introduction to a new song, the mood changed. When Bono told the crowd the next song was about Northern Ireland, things got a little tense. He was careful to point out that it was not a rebel song, and if they didn't like it the band would never play it in Belfast again. But by the end of "Sunday Bloody Sunday," the crowd had a new U2 live favorite and understood the true intentions of its message. There was an affirming, relief-releasing cheer.

To be from Dublin and title a song "Sunday Bloody Sunday" was asking for misinterpretation. Bloody Sunday was the name given to two of the darkest dates in Ireland's bloody history. One is

January 30, 1972—the day British troops shot and killed thirteen people during a civil rights march in nationalist Derry in Northern Ireland. The army has said it was shot at first. The civil rights marchers and the families of the dead have always disputed this, saying the victims were innocent. It fanned the flames of the area's troubles. In 2000, a fresh inquiry began to look again at the evidence of what happened. This memorable and controversial event even caused John Lennon to release a song of the same name on 1972's *Some Time In New York City* album along with another anti-British anthem "The Luck of the Irish."

Bloody Sunday was also the name of another tragic day in Dublin. On November 21, 1921, the British—in the form of the Regular Royal Irish Constabulary and the ruthless auxiliary the Black and Tans—entered Croke Park, the headquarters for the Gaelic Athletic Association. The association often was accused of being affiliated with Republicans, and the British shot and killed twelve people. The operation was carried out in retaliation for the IRA murdering fourteen British undercover agents in their beds. In recent years, this event became a crucial part of the film *Michael Collins* starring Liam Neeson.

Bono has always said that though Dublin was removed from the epicenter of the bombing and killing in the 1969-1994 troubles, it was where most of the bombs were made, and therefore he was unable to ignore it and had a right to speak out. He has made it clear that he had hopes for a united Ireland, something most evangelical Christians in Northern Ireland would oppose. But he has always made his stand against the violence.

There were, of course, those who misunderstood "Sunday Bloody

WALK ON

04

Sunday." The band got into trouble on both sides of the political divide. The Protestants were displeased with the seeming glorification of Bloody Sunday, which the Nationalists had been using as propaganda against the British troops. The Republicans were unhappy that the band was condemning the violence and therefore taking an anti-IRA stance.

Perhaps it was touring the world and getting away from the idealistic walls of the Shalom fellowship that caused the band to begin looking out.

SUNDAY BLOODY SUNDAY

Even amidst its political overtones, "Sunday Bloody Sunday" is also one of the more Christian statements on *War*. The band members bring in the prophet Isaiah and the Psalmist when they ask, "*How long must we sing this song?*" This line is reprised in their version of Psalm 40 at the end of the album. They also take the idea of blood and war back to the "*victory that Jesus won*" (John 20:1-9). Connecting these acts of bloody violence across the centuries to that first Palestinian Easter was in some sense pointing to their Christian faith as an answer to the problems of the North.

"Sunday Bloody Sunday" was the most successful moment on *War*. It is an inflammatory title, which is why Bono had to clarify that it isn't a rebel song. "Rebel" had Republican connotations in the Irish conflict. Instead, "Sunday Bloody Sunday" is an anti-war song, an ideal opening track for an album called *War*. It was a big first step into confrontational politics for the band and was a sign of the hard-edged political commentary to come.

If the eighties would be looked back upon as the flag-waving, stance-shouting, political activist phase of U2, the fact is there was little social activism in the band until this album. Prior to *War*, U2 concentrated on the soul, the spirit and the heart. Apart from perhaps "Stranger in a Strange Land" on *October*, there was nothing outward-looking until *War*, when it seems the band began dabbling in world events. Perhaps it was touring the world and getting away from the idealistic walls of the Shalom fellow-ship that caused the band to begin looking out. A couple of years later, Bono would tell *Hot Press*: "We grew up in an odd way as people...We were completely occupied with spiritual things...We weren't even sure we wanted to be in a band. So we were interested in growing on spiritual levels but quite retarded on other levels." [1]

The title track of *October* was probably the border checkpoint into *War*. There was a cold and bleak peering out to the king-doms rising and falling in a world that was by no means kind or tender. On the cover of *War*, album cover boy Peter Rowan's face looks fearfully aware. This was a change from the naiveté por-trayed on *Boy*. The band shots were set in snow that seemed to be nudging toward the harsh chill of Siberia rather than the pleasures of Colorado. These were all signs that these formerly parochial Dublin boys had begun to notice all was not well with the world.

As a first foray into such issues, it could be said that *War* was a naive realization and the album suffers in depth of content. But "Sunday Bloody Sunday" still stands as one of U2's best. The song was a constant in the band's live set and probably had its definitive rendering on a night that marked another dark day in the North's history. On Remembrance Sunday, November 8, 1987, the IRA exploded a bomb at the War Memorial in Enniskillen, Co., Fermanagh. Whether it was meant for the British forces or not, it killed thirteen innocent people and is probably best remembered for one of the better stories to come out of such murderous brutality. A man named Gordon Wilson was standing with his daughter, Marie, when the bomb went off. She was buried beneath the rubble and died holding his hand and telling him she loved him. The poignancy of those dying moments touched the world. His courageous and radical response to the loss of his daughter—forgiving the killers immediately—made him a symbol of new possibilities in Ireland. He campaigned for peace and reconciliation and even gained a place in the Republic of Ireland's senate.

On the night of the bombing, U2 was giving a concert in Denver, Colorado. In the middle of "Sunday Bloody Sunday," Bono, emotional from the day, ranted about how brave it was to kill children and old men who had just cleaned up their medals for the day. "F*** the revolution" was Bono's conclusion. Never before had the song's opening lines, "*I can't believe the news today/ I can't close my eyes and make it go away,*" been more apt. The band didn't play the song again until the end of the Popmart tour almost ten years later because it could never really escape that day in 1987.

WALK ON

04

U2 has always had a glimpse north in its political activism. IRA leader Gerry Adams and Rev. Ian Paisley, a fundamentalist born-again anti-Catholic preacher, joined David Trimble of the pre-dominantly Protestant Unionist Party (Ulster Unionist Party) and John Hume from the predominantly Catholic Nationalist Party (Social, Democratic and Labor Party) on the cover of the "Please" single. This sent a message to all the people of the North to please give us peace. The marching bands on "Wake Up Dead Man" on *Pop* also pointed to the nonsense that divides and costs lives. Every July, the traditionally Protestant marching sea-son (a cultural parallel to Morris Dancing in England) enflames the country. The Orange Order, a supposedly Christian order, wants to march the routes it has marched for hundreds of years. These roads, through demographic change, have become pre-dominantly Roman Catholic—the people the Orange Order is celebrating victory over in the march. The trenches dug within our hearts that U2 sang about on "Sunday Bloody Sunday" have caused bitter, irreconcilable stand-offs, violence and civil disorder.

Of course, Ireland has continued to be on U2's agenda right up to the present, when "Peace on Earth" on *All That You Can't Leave Behind* was written as an angry exorcism to another all too simi-lar event—the Omagh bombing. On Saturday afternoon, August 15, 1998, in the little market town of Omagh, Tyrone County, twenty-nine shoppers were blown to pieces and scores more were maimed for life. This happened not far up the road from Enniskillen. A renegade terrorist organization called the Real IRA, which was opposed to the IRA's ceasefire and involvement in the peace process, claimed responsibility. It was Northern Ireland's darkest day and garnered the highest death toll in the four decades of such bombings. And it happened during what was supposedly peace time.

The Omagh bombing impacted Bono, as it did the whole country, more than most of the horrendous things that have been done on the little island that Bono's father used to tell him was just sod to keep your feet from getting wet. The story goes that Bono wrote the words of "Peace on Earth" the night after it occurred. The fact that the bomb exploded in August and the title of the song is taken from the biblical Christmas story makes little difference to its impact.

Perhaps what made the Omagh bombing even more painful to Bono was that he and the band had been part of the peace process that seemed to have been shattered that day. Since Bloody Sunday and Enniskillen, something miraculous had been happening in Northern Ireland. The Republican and Loyalist terrorists had declared ceasefires at the end of August 1994, and though a bombing in London in March 1996 interrupted the peace progress, another ceasefire led the way to a momentous Good Friday agreement in 1998. Almost all of the political parties signed an agreement that would look at local government reforms—from the police service to the decommissioning of weapons and more—that would build a platform to a lasting solution to hundreds of years of hostility.

There was to be a referendum in May 1998. The people of both the Republic of Ireland and Northern Ireland would vote on the agreement. Leading up to the vote, some of the anti-agreement parties had been trying to convince the people that this was a sell-out to terrorism and to vote no. Some of the strongest arguments came from evangelical Christians who supposedly fol-

WALK ON

04

lowed a Bible that teaches them "to make every effort to live at peace with all men" (Heb. 12:14) and to "love their enemies and do good to those who persecute you" (Luke 6:27, 28).

> "I want it all, and I want it now. Heaven on earth—now—let's have a bit of that."
>
> — SUNDAY BLOODY SUNDAY

Days before the vote, there was a "Yes" Campaign concert to reach young voters and get publicity in Belfast's new pride and joy, The Waterfront Hall. Ash, a local rock music success story, was to play. On stage, the leaders of the two sides of the community—Trimble of the Protestant Unionist Party and Hume of the Catholic Nationalist Party—would appear together. What put the icing on the cake was U2 agreeing to make an appearance. U2 had offered its services to northern groups before but had always stipulated that it needed to be across the divide. At last, here was the country's greatest opportunity.

Many watched the events on television. After a version of The Beatles' "Don't Let Me Down," Bono told the crowd: "It's great to be in Belfast in a week where history is being made. I would like to introduce two men who are making history. Two men who have taken a leap of faith, out of the past and into the future."

Hume and Trimble walked out, and Bono held both their hands up to a loudly affirming crowd. It was a moment that many watched in utter disbelief. It was a defining moment in history. It was a moment of grace. U2 had brought that "victory Jesus won" into a tangible reality. Seventy-one percent of the people in Northern Ireland took the leap of faith with Hume and Trimble. The future was filled with hope, and U2's role in this should not be underestimated. In her balanced and informative book *Northern Protestants: An Unsettled People*, Susan McKay describes the two men holding Bono's hands: "They looked awkward, but it was a winning gesture which had revived a floundering campaign." [2]

Hence Bono's consternation when he played the two poignant songs "North and South of the River" and "All I Want Is You" for a Remembrance Day special for the Omagh bombing victims on the Republic of Ireland's national television channel six months later. "North and South of the River," which could be seen as a grown-up "Sunday Bloody Sunday," has profound lyrics and was written with a legend in Ireland, folk singer Christy Moore. It first appeared on Moore's *Graffiti Tongue* album a year before U2's minimalist version became the B side of "Staring at the Sun."

The folk tradition where Moore has been a superstar for three decades has been known as a place of Republican propaganda. Moore himself supported the IRA's armed struggle for many years but turned his back on it around the time of the Enniskillen bomb. In this co-write with Bono and The Edge, there is an awareness that religion has led minds astray, and there is yearning for repentance, reconciliation and mutual

WALK ON

04

understanding without any need for surrender—a reference to the clarion call of Ulster Protestants: "No Surrender!" The lines that became most powerful and poignant as U2 performed the song for the TV special were, "*'Cause there's no feeling that's so alone/ As when the one you're hurting is your own.*" There are also fragments of hope in the midst of the evil: "*There was a badness that had its way/ But love wasn't lost/ Love will have its day.*" "All I Want Is You" moved from a yearning for love in a romantic sense to a lament for those who lost loved ones in the bombing. Omagh was the only bombing in memory where everyone in Ireland felt they lost someone. Northern Ireland has a tiny population of 1.5 million people, and that afternoon everyone in the country feared they lost a friend. The entire population listened fearfully to news reports for names and wondered about friends who might have been in Omagh town center that day. Bono sang for everyone, but especially the families of the murdered: "*You say you want to find some peace/ You say you want to see her face/ And this hatred will get us no place/ All the promises you made/ From the cradle to the grave/ When all I want is you.*" Those promises looked back to that Good Friday agreement, to that moment in the Waterfront Hall and to that resulting referendum.

U2 believes that the Gospel of Jesus Christ has an agenda for peacemaking and justice and a Kingdom coming. They also believe that Kingdom could come now on this side of eternity. As Bono said in *Hot Press* at the end of 1988: "I don't expect this pie in the sky when you die stuff. My favorite line in the Lord's Prayer is 'Thy Kingdom come, Thy will be done on earth as it is in heaven' (Matt. 6:10). I want it all, and I want it now. Heaven on earth—now—let's have a bit of that." [3]

As the band dusted "Sunday Bloody Sunday" off for the Elevation tour in 2001, the song had become a celebration of the positive, if cautious, steps Northern Ireland had taken toward a lasting peace. During the Pittsburgh concert of the Elevation tour in 2001, Bono introduced the song by telling the crowd, "If you're Irish, you got something to sing about on this song." It is as if there has been a change from the shame of the Irish situation to almost a pride in what had been achieved. As someone passed him an Irish flag during the song, he acknowledged, "There was a time when you couldn't hold this flag so high." The peace process was again in jeopardy as U2 set out on the UK leg of the Elevation tour. Bono threw his encouragement to the politicians across the Irish sea when he told the crowd in Manchester, "Our prayer is that this week brave people make brave decisions, and this little island does not go back to war...Compromise is not such a bad word after all." The chant at the end of "Sunday Bloody Sunday" had changed in the new hopeful, if fragile, climate. Instead of the screaming of "no more, no more" at the end of the song, Bono invited the crowd to "sing into the presence of love, sing into the presence of peace." There was a hope that these words would be sung for a long time.

LIVE AID

July 13, 1985, was an unforgettable day in U2's history. Still on the cusp of success, the band took the stage on Wembley's Live Aid bill at 5:20 in the afternoon. It was five hours before the event's finale, a signal of U2's still up-and-coming status at the time. Perhaps it was this day that launched the band into the next stratosphere of success. As Bono's natural charisma mingled with the emotion of the day to flood his body with big-stadium adrenalin, he decided to bridge the gap between the stars and the people. In one of the most memorable moments of the day, he pulled some girls out of the crowd and slow-danced with them before millions of viewers worldwide. Somehow, in one of the biggest and widest television audiences ever, he made the dance feel intimate. Fan and performer united in the day that rock music changed the world.

The spontaneity of the dance cost U2 a song that night. "Pride," which was to be the band's last song and was the crowd favorite at the time, had to be sacrificed. However, only playing two songs—"Bad" and "Sunday Bloody Sunday"—didn't affect the band's sales, which tripled in the coming months. The band's live reputation was enhanced beyond measure, yet Bono left Wembley shattered by the experience. Perhaps the contradictions of the day were on the mind of this young, emotional, deep thinker. Was there not something incongruous about a great rock celebration aiding people who were starving to death? That might have been part of the cause of Bono's post-gig depression. But he also seems to have felt his dancing embarrassed the band. He actually took off by himself around Ireland to come to terms with it, maybe on a similar soul search as when the band had considered giving up around October. Somewhere in west Ireland, the story goes, Bono met a sculptor who was working on a piece called "The Leap," inspired by Bono's moment of letting go. It was quite a symbol on all kinds of levels for the band, the industry and mankind. The leap at the crux of Bono's 2000 movie *Million Dollar Hotel* may have begun here.

Of course, Live Aid was not about Bono's personal journey, nor was it about selling more albums or enhancing the band's reputation. That may have been the view of the cynics. But if rock music ever laid its ego down for a day, this was it. For U2, Live Aid reinforced the band's belief that music could change the world. As a result of the Band Aid and Live Aid projects, Bono and his wife, Ali, went to Ethiopia in 1985. This event had a marked effect on both of their lives, as well as the band's music.

In some ways, it was at this point U2 began to take over the mantle of the folk, pop and rock protest movement that traces its roots back to Woody Guthrie, Bob Dylan, John Lennon and even

Boomtown Rats' Bob Geldof. Funny enough, in his band's first single Geldof sang, "*I don't want no charity; all I want is me.*" It's ironic how the punk rocker from Dublin who sang about looking after number one selflessly fed the world, while those who say "love your neighbor as yourself" (Luke 10:25-37) only look after number one. Geldof himself would say that God looked down and saw he who was least likely and decided to use him. Maybe in that light, Band Aid was meant to embarrass the Church.

It is John Lennon who has been Bono's soul mate from beyond the grave. Lennon always has been a big influence on Bono's music and life. Bono once said of Lennon, "For somebody like myself, John Lennon really did kind of write the rule book...As a tunesmith, as an irritant, as a willing taker of pratfalls." [1] That they hold a spiritual affinity even though Lennon never had much faith in God may seem a little unfitting, but true. U2's "God Part 2" was, in some ways, meant to bring the atheist viewpoint together with the Christian believers.

Bono and Lennon's connection was more in their honesty and desire that the platform of music be used to change the world. More than using the injustices around them to stoke the fires of their songwriting, they wanted to get out there and bring on the revolution. Of course, Lennon was part of the great hippy idealism of the sixties, and there was a belief that flower power could instigate a new world. Sociologist and Christian writer Tony Campolo suggests in his book *Who Switched the Price Tags* that the hippies of the late sixties had much in common with the Kingdom of God. He writes: "While they were arrogant and haughty, they did seem to have the right kind of dreams. As a matter of fact, in their idealism, I found values that I wished were more evident in the churches I attended and served. There was something noble about their visions of the future, and those of us committed to a radical theology of the Kingdom of God began to think that these young people were more Christian than those who filled the pews of churches…Those long-haired males and braless females possessed a childlike innocence that made them seem exceedingly fit for the Kingdom of heaven." [2]

Lennon's much-publicized bed-in for peace spawned his song "Give Peace a Chance." A few years later, he released *Some Time in New York City*, a political manifesto that touched on feminism, and support for the Black Panther movement and the Irish terror group the IRA. It could be said that *War* was an early, naive and youthful attempt by U2 to write and record a *Some Time in New York City*-type album. There was a look at global issues and, of course, "Sunday Bloody Sunday." Lennon's was a more vehement attack on the British soldiers and their policy in Northern Ireland—a less peaceful rage than U2's. For sure, Lennon was the artist who encouraged the young U2 to look out.

From *War* on, U2 began to become a politically active, cause-carrying, justice-driven band. In 1987, just after the release of *The Joshua Tree*, Niall Stokes commented on the changes in U2: "One thing is that Bono has become far more political. There was a time when a discussion of politics would have seemed irrelevant to him. He was more interested in spiritual issues. Now they have become more political, and the new album is an awareness of that." [3]

This new campaigning heart was in no way a change in perspective for the band. It was not that the members had left spiritual issues behind. They were not replacing one with another. Rather, they were opening up their spiritual quest to take in all that their faith was about. Bono said in 1988: "To me, faith in Jesus Christ that is not aligned to social justice—that is not aligned with the poor—it's nothing." [4]

Their faith went this direction for many reasons. Leaving the insular shelter of Dublin in the late seventies and stepping out onto the world stage was magnified by the band's being asked to take part in the Band Aid single in late 1984. Boomtown Rats' Bob Geldof, one of the few success stories to come out of Dublin before U2, had seen the horrific pictures of the famine in

"To me, faith in Jesus Christ that is not aligned to social justice—that is not aligned with the poor—it's nothing."

LIVE AID

Ethiopia on the news in late 1984. He was so moved, he phoned his mate from Ultravox, Midge Ure, and the two wrote a song. They got several pop stars to sing a line in the song, and they made it into the top-selling single of all time in the UK. The proceeds from that song went to famine relief. Bono got the God line: "*Well tonight, thank God it's them instead of you.*"

WALK ON

05

It was around this time that U2 began to give their whole-heart-ed support to Amnesty International. Bono campaigned for vic-tims of injustice around the world. He later said one of the things he was most proud of in his career was highlighting the work of this charity in his music. U2 always would give space on its album sleeves to highlight a few cases and give details on how to join the organization. U2 was part of the Conspiracy of Hope tour in 1986, as was Sting, Peter Gabriel, Lou Reed, Bryan Adams and others. The tour across America promoted the organization's mission.

For some reason, many Christians were suspicious of the band's political awareness. They feared it was another sign of moving away from the heart of the Gospel. Was U2 ashamed of the Gospel that it had proclaimed so vigorously on October to be going on and on now about social issues? Evangelical Christianity seems to have forgotten that Jesus asked His disci-ples to do just what U2 was doing. In one situation, Jesus told His followers that if they wanted to know who was going to heaven, they just had to look at who fed the poor and visited the sick or the prisoners. He said those people were doing those things unto Christ Himself, as He was manifested in "the least of these" (Matt. 25:31-46).

Many Christians find comfort on Sunday mornings in the Bible verse that says where two or three are gathered in Jesus' name, He is there with them (Matt. 18:20). For some reason, they pre-fer that verse over the one that says the prisoner and the tramp in the street is Jesus, too. When it comes to which place Jesus would prefer to be met, you have to wonder. Would He rather see His Kingdom come by His followers praying for His

Kingdom to come, or by them putting their faith into action? Perhaps in working to bring social justice and compassion to the world, the members of U2 were more certain of their place in heaven than when they just talked about it.

Jesus wasn't the only one in the Bible who saw social justice as the vital manifestation of the life of faith. The prophets, particularly Amos, suggested that God was not interested in their song of worship or their holy days or their spiritual gatherings unless "justice flowed like a river and righteousness like an ever-flowing stream" (Amos 5:24). Far from being a move away from their faith, U2's political activism was in keeping with it. Maybe in those seeming throwaway lines from "Please" on *Pop* where Bono cries *"Please, please get up off your knees,"* he was asking the Church to get out of prayer meetings and into the everyday dirt and pain of bringing the Kingdom. That is what this band believed in: *"I believe in the Kingdom come/ Where all the colors will bleed into one/ And yes I'm still running..."* And run they will until they have found here on earth how it is in heaven—what they are looking for.

FOR THE REV. MARTIN LUTHER KING—SING!

When Bono joined Bob Dylan onstage at Slane Castle for a memorable performance on a sunny Sunday in July 1984, he did so as the underdog. U2 was at the top of its class, but the band had not yet graduated to the level of the great Dylan. As Bono bluffed his way through Dylan's "Leopard Skin Pillbox Hat" and improvised the words to "Blowing in the Wind," no one knew U2 was actually in the process of making the album that would propel their journey to greatness.

The band's most recent album at the time, *Under a Blood Red Sky*, released in late 1983. With its accompanying video, the band seemed to have mastered its show—The Edge's chunky, chiming guitar perfectly balancing Bono's prancing, posing, flag-waving and high-powered emotion. This was a group that had become good at what it did. But at the same time, the band members realized that to get better they would need to leave behind the security of repeating proven formulas.

1984's *The Unforgettable Fire* was U2's first reinvention. It was also the band's first album after they decided their faith could live alongside their art. If this album showed anything, it was that. The band realized that cliché-ridden Christian couplets were not necessary or helpful in their sharing their faith. Being impressionistic would do. They were artists, not missionaries, in a proclamation sense.

Bill Graham put it well when he said, "Insofar as the album is Christian, the Holy Spirit is the presiding member of the trinity." [1] There is a spiritual feel to the piece. *The Unforgettable Fire* seems to describe the thin places where heaven and earth are so close that you can almost scratch some of the gold off the streets of glory. Graham also describes the album as "a travelogue of the soul." [2]

Given this, *The Unforgettable Fire* was a bold shift in direction— which would become a trait of the band. The guys of U2 made some brave decisions, throwing themselves into a deeper sea where the first question was always, *Can they avoid drowning?* Choosing Brian Eno as producer was radical. Eno had been a member of Roxy Music and producer for Talking Heads and David Bowie, but he had never so much as heard any of U2's material. Initially, Eno turned down the band's request. He finally agreed and brought to the equation Canadian Daniel Lanois. This set in place a team that would collaborate on some of the strongest music of the next fifteen years.

The Unforgettable Fire was a mysterious, meandering album. It was big, big music and had Lanois' and Eno's imprint all over it. In a word, it was impressionistic. Though it still has The Edge's trademark guitar shuffling and scuttling along, it is a much more mature performance by the band. Bono's lyrics were just lines and poetic shades whose meaning rarely extended beyond each couplet. The themes of hope, home, belief and giving away were all there, but there was little in the way of clear statements of faith, as on *October*, or of the world, as on *War*. Of course, there was "Pride (In the Name of Love)" which became U2's biggest hit to date and apart from "Bad" is the only song on the album that still rates in the U2 classic canon. It perhaps remains the band's trademark song, with the anthemic sound, spiritual core and political edge. It also happens to be the only song on the album where the title is in the lyrics.

"Pride" and the album title *The Unforgettable Fire* were both inspired by a trip to The Chicago Peace Museum. A series of paintings and drawings by survivors of the Hiroshima and Nagasaki holocaust at the end of World War II was on display, and the title of the exhibition immediately struck Bono as a good name for U2's next album.

While at the museum, the band saw another exhibit dedicated to the life and campaigning of Dr. Martin Luther King, Jr. The guys immediately felt empathy for him. In their lives, as well as in "Sunday Bloody Sunday," they advocated pacifism. King's belief in non-violence was something they would echo in all their political campaigning. They had expressed hope that a Martin Luther King would emerge in the Northern Ireland troubles.

King was an interesting hero of the band at this stage of its spiritual development. As the members of U2 had been exposed to more of the world and more of what masquerades as

"Christian," there was much heart- and soul-searching. They were looking for new definitions of the faith they had taken hold of in their teens. There were new questions and realities, and they were deciding what to toss out from the baggage of their past Christian experience and what to hold onto. This was many believers' experience. After a time of dealing with the inner soul, being almost nurtured on milk, as the apostle Paul puts it in one of his epistles, born again gives way to growing up again, and the world of the adult takes on very different issues than that of the infant.

As the band members were discarding some of their role models from Shalom and finding it hard to involve themselves with another local group of believers as such, a figure like King and his writings, thoughts and behavior was just what the soul doctor prescribed. He was someone to look up to. He was someone to help them sort out their questions. He, in some ways, was a Christ figure who gave himself for the betterment of others. His politics and investigative spirituality where he was not afraid to question the givens of the evangelical world in which he was brought up were things to which the Christian in U2 could relate. His writings were far more inspirational than to just give them two great songs.

Yet two great songs they got. The song "MLK" took the same role on the album that "40" had on *War*—the haunting, moody finale. It was a song of deep sadness as it reflected on the tragedy of King's death. Almost the opposite of "MLK" was "Pride," which was all about celebration in spite of King's assassination because his death was not the end of his life or his cause. His soul and his pride and his victory could not be taken away.

That Bono's words took a step back from the soapbox proclamation of his earlier work was due largely to the fact the band had become suspicious of right-wing American evangelicalism. Bono

> "I go to America and I turn on my television set, and I start sweating profusely because those guys have turned faith into an industry. It's appalling."
>
> — FOR THE REV. MARTIN LUTHER KING—SING

would talk about this quite a lot in the years to come. He told Robert Hillman in 1987: "I go to America and I turn on my television set, and I start sweating profusely because those guys have turned faith into an industry. It's appalling. It's ugly—the guy's hand is virtually coming out of the television set." [3]

The Unforgettable Fire was the band's first post-Shalom fellowship release, and the guys would never have a very healthy relationship with the Church again. Of course, they have not exactly lived a life that is very conducive to church commitment. Around the time they left Shalom, they were becoming one of the world's busiest rock bands. Their schedule did not make it too easy for them to attend church regularly. And their fame made it hard for them to slip into the back pew unnoticed. Bono has said that even if he could and wanted to attend church on a regular basis, it would become the biggest church in Dublin—not

WALK ON

06

because of anything God was doing but because of his being there.

A few years later in the song "Acrobat," on 1991's *Achtung Baby*, it seems Bono admitted to his loss of not having a place of regular liturgy, creed and accountability. He sings, *"And I'd join the move-ment/ If there was one I could believe in/ Yeah, I'd break the bread and wine/ If there was a church I could receive in."* The song contin-ues as a confession of Bono's devoutness: *"And I must be an acro-bat/ To talk like this/ And act like that."* Bono, as he is never afraid to do, shows a vulnerable, honest side. He is almost embarrassed that his thought and art are so rooted in the Christian faith, yet his actions don't live up to the belief.

Bono has returned to this idea again and again over the years. He has spoken of not being a great example of the Christian faith. He has made many references to having been drawn to peace-makers like Ghandi, King and Christ not because he has himself been by nature a pacifist, but because he has been the opposite. He told Liam Mackey in 1988: "The reason I'm attracted to the light of Scriptures is because there's another side of me that is dark. The reason I'm interested in men of peace is because I'm not like them and would like to be. I'm not someone in real life who turns the other cheek." [4] (Matt. 5:39)

Twelve years later, he takes up the same thread in a *Q* magazine interview. In it, he says: "I get discouraged by my base emotions. I write songs about high ideals and aspirations, and I admire Martin Luther King and John Hume, peaceful people, but ... I'm capable of aggression of a really brutal kind. If that rears its head and I give in to it and thump somebody, then I feel really low." [5]

He goes on, "I wish I could live up to Christianity. It's like I'm a fan; I'm not actually in the band." This is the same Christian who told Joe Jackson while discussing Elvis' demise: "I think it was guilt that made Elvis lose the will to live. Yet in the Scripture there is another line: 'There is, therefore no condemnation for those who are in God' (Rom. 8:1). There is no guilt. Guilt is not of God. It is false teaching." [6]

This seems to be a normal response to the contradictions that any believer experiences between the idealism of what can be achieved in the cross, the resurrection of Christ and the outpouring of the Holy Spirit, and the sometimes slow progress in attaining it. In Ireland there is a lot of talk about Catholic guilt, when someone who partakes in Mass on Sunday lives a life devoid of that spiritual belief the rest of the week. There is a similar Protestant guilt that lurks in the temples of those who claim to be free from having to earn their salvation by works. There are always expectations of behavioral codes and ecclesiastical dues that when not achieved or even sought leave us feeling that salvation is either lost or not as sure-footed as it was.

Evangelicals believe they are saved by grace through faith (Eph. 2:8, 9) but then add a man-made waiver that you have to work as hard as you can to meet middle class behavioral patterns to hang onto it. It seems to be contrary to the Gospel, where among the many teachings of Jesus regarding servanthood, the last become first. It is an upside-down Kingdom contradicting what seems the natural order of the first being first and the best winning. The Church therefore should be radically opposed to such a success syndrome. It seems this affected Bono. Another strange quirk about the Church is it has specific qualities that

WALK ON

indicate whether you are an "acrobat." Usually, they have to do with swearing, smoking and drinking. For some reason, there are biblical teachings that do not—but perhaps should—hold so much importance. Among them: materialistic greed, bigoted prejudice, the oppression of women or the neglect of social justice. Somehow you can ignore many of the rallying calls of Christ and the prophets, and because you are teetotal and less flowery with your language and attend church twice a week, you are declared spiritually strong.

> "Religion has torn this country apart. I have no time for it, and I never felt a part of it. I am a Christian, but at times I feel very removed from Christianity."
>
> — FOR THE REV. MARTIN LUTHER KING—SING

Bono speaks of grace being the great attraction to Christianity. Then he says he'd like to be a Christian but could never shape up or that he is a bad example of Christianity. Either he is trying to deflect the press's ability to pigeon-hole him, or he has been duped about what a Christian is. Like his critics, he misses his committed and radical following of Jesus in things such as giving an enormous amount of his time to Jubilee 2000. He pushed back his career and new album by more than a year to try to rid the Third World of crippling debts, keep the poor alive, and restore equality and justice to the world. And he says he is not a good example for Christ. Jesus told a parable about the Kingdom of God where the sheep enter the Kingdom, and the goats are left outside (Matt. 25:31-46). Jesus didn't say the goats smoked, drank or swore too much. He said they didn't get involved in changing the circumstances of the marginalized by feeding them when they were hungry and visiting them in prison. These were the issues of His Kingdom.

When it comes to the dilemma of the Catholic and Protestant guilt complexes, it needs to be remembered that Bono is both and, at the same time, neither. He has consistently talked of how he despises religion but is a great believer in Christ. For Bono, The Edge and Larry, the God that they met and have pilgrimaged with down the amazing road is a God who is bigger than Church or religious boundaries. They discovered Him outside of the straight jacket of traditional religion, and they have continued to see a God Who has gotten bigger and bigger in every way.

In 1990, at the Greenbelt Arts Festival in England, rock journalist, biographer and poet Steve Turner did a seminar on how the Church was not good at being involved in conversations in the real world. He spoke of how many believers were not involved in the world at all and saw it as a bad place, not a place where Christians should be. Other believers were uninformed. They ran headlong into the world with clichéd religious slogans that made sense in church but were not understood outside it. These believers didn't relate in any ways that were understood or relevant. The third group consisted of believers who were unintegrated. They were involved in the culture but were so cut off from the Christian Church that they just blended in and thus made no impression.

Turner has used U2 as an example of a rock band that had been involved successfully in the conversation going on in the band's little corner of the vineyard. Turner co-wrote the official book for the movie *Rattle and Hum* [7] with Pete Williams and included a lengthy spiritual insight into the band in his book *Hungry for Heaven.* [8] There is little doubt that due to circumstances outside the band's control, U2 could have ended up among the unintegrated. Turner said not only did U2 get involved in that conversation at the cutting edge of the rock world, but the band even changed the language of the conversation. As one example, he asked if Simple Minds would have ever recorded a song like "Sanctify Yourself" before U2 got in among rock's movers and shakers and started using religious imagery.

In Turner's analysis, where U2 would always be in danger would be in their integration. For Bono, Larry and The Edge, their church has had to be the "coffee table fellowship," or dare I say "the barstool fellowship." They have kept their spiritual dialogue going through friends who share their faith, whether that might be old friends in Dublin, or fellow musicians such as T-Bone Burnett or Bruce Cockburn, or journalists and writers such as Turner. There have always been fellow believers involved within U2's inner circle professionally, artistically and socially.

Probably most significantly, Bono has been able to sharpen his faith and continue to get inspired about his spiritual worldview by opening himself to "fellowship" with those who do not share his Christian viewpoint. He is always open to talk about the Christian faith with whoever will listen. Though they have been known to attend churches locally or around the world on various occasions, they have been mainly limited to these informal means of spiritual nourishment and accountability.

U2's lack of integration with the Church is not entirely due to their fame and itinerant lifestyle, though. The band took a huge step back from Christian structures around the time of *War* and *The Unforgettable Fire*. Bono would say at the time: "Well, religion has torn this country apart. I have no time for it, and I never felt a part of it. I am a Christian, but at times I feel very removed from Christianity. The Jesus Christ I believe in was the man who turned over the tables in the temple and threw the moneychangers out—substitute TV evangelists if you like. There is a radical side to Christianity that I am attracted to. And I think without a commitment to social justice, it is empty ... When I see these racketeers, the snake-oil salesmen on these right-wing television stations, asking not for your $20 or your $50, but your $100 in the name of Jesus Christ, I just want to throw up." [9]

According to that statement, there is another reason for the band members' stepping back. After *October*, they openly quoted Scripture and happily confessed their faith during several interviews. This was when they were most intensely involved with Shalom, and coming from their sheltered Christian base in Dublin, they were fairly unaware of what born-again Christianity meant throughout the rest of the world. They would soon find out. During a tour of the United States not long after the *October* publicity campaign, they came across a brand of evangelicalism that they simply could not understand or stomach. As Bono says, it made them want to throw up. They also began to realize that when they stated their Christian belief in the music press, people were equating what they were saying with right-wing, fundamentalist Christians in America. U2 was unhappy with such a com-

WALK ON

parison and stood back from it. This was why the guys quit
being so open with the press about the definitions of their faith.
It was not a silence imposed by Island Records for commercial
reasons. It was the right-wing Church that was forcing them to
shut up. But they never really did.

Not only did they stand back from such right-wing churches,
they started to criticize them openly in interviews and from the
stage. To some, this may have been seen as a betrayal of their
previous spiritual allegiance. The band probably would have
seen it as developing that allegiance. As they shone the light of
their faith across the world to critique politics and make a stand
for justice and change, they would shine that beam of truth
across the Church, too, to illuminate the dross that has caused
its decay.

This could be seen on the *Rattle and Hum* movie, when Bono, in
one of his characteristic monologues, ends "Bullet the Blue Sky,"
which is about American foreign policy in Central America, with:
"But I see no difference between the CBS News and Hill Street
Blues and a preacher on The Old Time Gospel Hour stealing
money from the sick and the old. Well, the God I believe in isn't
short of cash, mister!" The link between televangelists, right-wing
fundamentalism and the bombing of innocent people in El
Salvador was a potent cocktail of prophetic anger.

In 1994, The Edge said to John Waters, "We probably, at this
point, have deeply disappointed a lot of Christians because what
I perceive as freedom, they would perceive as complete decadence and self-indulgence." [10] This shows that U2 is aware of the
wariness with which the Christian world looks upon the band,

but the three Christians in the band lose no sleep over such opinions. There was a point in their career when they made a conscious decision to deflect any kind of allegiance to conservative evangelical Christianity and attempted to break that mass movement from giving any allegiance to them. There may be many reasons for this break, but it's important to remember that U2 has never denied its allegiance with Christ. That some have not been happy with the outworking of such a confession does not negate what the band members believe.

It might be that the members of U2 had to distance themselves from the Church to be able to be faithful to their sense of vocation. There are hints here of the messianic secret of the Gospels. There are many recorded instances in the Gospel accounts of Jesus' life where He told his disciples and people he had healed not to tell people who He was (Luke 9:21). The reason was that if people knew, they would put the wrong expectations on Him and draw Him away from the heart of his vocation. U2's vocation was in no way messianic, but that evangelical Christians' expectations might distract the band from its vocation was a danger. Maybe what U2 has achieved for God has been as a result of not being tied to any particular denomination. So many of those who try to take Christ into the world, whether it be as missionaries or artists, are tied by those who look over their shoulders. There is a lot of peer pressure within churches or in Christian movements to dot all the i's and cross all the t's of a precise and perfect faith. The late Christian artist Rich Mullins had told audiences he once was not allowed to record a song because his record company felt it was not the sort of message the target audience would buy.

By being outside the pressures of Church expectations, U2 has been able to take risks and do its own thing. This is not an ideal scenario for any Christian, especially those facing the temptations and dilemmas of the rock world. But as a result of the uniqueness of the band's situation, it has been able to make a unique contribution to the culture without having to compromise it or water it down.

YOU KNOW I BELIEVE IT

The Joshua Tree was U2's finest moment. Until the album's release in 1987, the group had been all potential and promise. With *The Joshua Tree*, U2 achieved it. The album welcomed their status as rock legends. Yet as U2 sat at the top of the music charts around the world, the Christian community used the album's release as reason to write the band's spiritual obituary. One of the songs in particular sparked the backlash. It had the band's former Christian community in Dublin, as well as many believers around the world, mourning—and in some cases celebrating—the evidence that the band's days of being torch-bearers of Christian truth were over. "I Still Haven't Found What I'm Looking For" was a pivotal song in the band's artistic intentions and spiritual development. The Soul Patrol and Theological Police were out in force, though, and they concluded their case that anyone who had not found what they were looking for could not have found Christ.

It was a remarkable response that not only highlighted a shoddy piece of listening to the song's lyrics, but also showed a great error in what was masquerading in some quarters as Christianity. There seems to be a belief that once someone makes the initial connection with Jesus Christ, he has arrived. Immediately, a watertight box of solutions is handed to him. No more questions need to be asked—Jesus is the answer! Everything is now explained; there is nothing left to search for. This view is built on a need for precision and perfection, which has always been an enemy of art, which is all about coloring outside the lines. It is also an enemy of the reality that following Jesus is a journey, not an arrival.

The members of U2 knew what they were stirring up. By now, disillusioned with formal fellowships or churches of any kind and growing in their spiritual thinking, they were making a statement about a less dogmatic approach to their faith. Yet the dogma in the song is widespread. Even with the song's dichotomy, it could be regarded as their clearest confession of faith. Daniel Lanois spoke on "The Making of *The Joshua Tree*" video about having suggested that Bono write a gospel song. Up to that point, the band had been writing songs with Christian content. A gospel song was another category entirely, and Lanois seemed to have seen it as a natural place of inspiration for a band that was so wrapped up in all things Christian. Bono listened to his producer's advice and wrote "I Still Haven't Found What I'm Looking For," calling it "a gospel song for a restless spirit."

The Joshua Tree was the album on which Bono discovered the art of the song. Before this there had been a lot of impressionistic improvisation. But somewhere between *The Unforgettable Fire*

and *The Joshua Tree*, Bono began to hone his craft. It could have been that sharing stages with the likes of Dylan, Baez and Sting, and hanging out with great writers had provoked Bono to try and imitate his peers. Perhaps it was a new sense of belief in what the band was becoming. Whatever it was, *The Joshua Tree* took the experimentation of Eno and Lanois' *The Unforgettable Fire*, melted it into the tighter sounds of Lillywhite's first three albums and added more attention to lyrical detail. The result: "Our most literate record yet," [1] according to Bono. His focus on the song made "I Still Haven't Found What I'm Looking For" a concise creed of redemption: "*You broke the bonds/ You loosed the chains/ Carried the cross/ And my shame/ You know I believe it!*"

Redemption, atonement and the substitution death of Christ. There would be no more succinct a theology of the cross in all the songs that were coming from the Christian bands U2's Christian critics would hold as models of sound theological content. The band, which many condemned for not proclaiming the Gospel and being ashamed of it, could not have spelled it out more clearly or poetically. Surely, this is what the Church needed. Christians in the real world being salt and light (Matt. 5:13, 16)—and in this case with a dirty great big fog horn, proclaiming the faith with the attention of the nation if not the greater part of the world. The song held the number one position on the singles charts for more than a month.

Instead of being a rejection of faith, "I Still Haven't Found What I'm Looking For" is an indication that U2 might have been closer to biblical truth than the narrow and precise Christians that pointed their finger. In the book *The Post-Evangelical*, English vicar Dave Tomlinson states: "Evangelicalism is good at introducing people to faith in Christ, but unhelpful when it comes to the matter of progressing into a more grown-up experience of faith." [2] Tomlinson may generalize, but it is true that the evangelical wing of the Church spends a lot of energy on being "born again" but little time on "growing up" again. There is a failing to encourage newborn believers out of the maternity ward and into a big

> "At one time, I thought you had to have all the answers if you were going to write a song, so it was embarrassing to make a record that was filled with doubts and questions."
>
> — YOU KNOW I BELIEVE IT

world where they will spend the rest of their spiritual lives trying to find what they are looking for.

The New Testament contains a letter from the apostle Paul to the church in Philippi (Phil. 3:4-16). Paul makes his beliefs clear. He tells the Philippians he has given up striving to get to God by being a religious Pharisee and has put his belief in the "righteousness that comes from God and is by faith." After years of working on some kind of way to God by adhering to his Jewish rituals, rules and regulations, he has set them aside and now believes in the Gospel that U2 so elegantly describes in its hit single. Paul could not find what he was looking for by being religious.

He says: "Not that I have already obtained all this, or have already been made perfect, but I press on to take hold of that for which Christ Jesus has taken hold of me…Forgetting what is behind and straining towards what is ahead, I press on." Paul had to take the belief, then go where that belief would lead him. Proclaiming a new doctrinal statement did not bring with it an overnight holiness. He had to keep "pressing on to the higher calling of my Lord," as Bob Dylan had paraphrased on his song "Pressing On" from his *Saved* album in 1980.

If Christians look at the events of the past few years in Rwanda, Angola, Mozambique, Sarajevo, the Middle East or Belfast City, they cannot say those tragedies are what they have been looking for. If they look at a Church filled with gossip, malicious lies in the name of truth, the bondage of legalism or the bigoted hypocrites who sometimes hold power, they can't say this is what they are looking for. As they look into their own lives and see the egotistical, selfish, sinful spouse, parent, child, workmate or friend, they can't say they have found what they are looking for. It is the realization that they haven't found what they are looking for that should draw them back to the only hope for being born again or growing up again: "*You broke the bonds, loosed the chains, carried the cross and my shame.*" It is only God's grace, through that work of redemption, that has brought them safe this far. And it is only His grace, through that work of redemption, that will lead them home. Until believers take that breath out of this world and into the hope-filled eternity of the next, they will be searching.

Bono's running and climbing and crawling toward "the Kingdom come where all the colors will bleed into one," and realizing that

WALK ON

07

as well as speaking in the tongues of angels he sometimes holds the hands of the devil, is perhaps a truer description of the pilgrimage of faith. Bono has been honest about his failings when it comes to his life and Christian journey. While the Church might ignore the darkness within and try to cover up its hangups with a shirt and tie, Bono has continually shown us himself, warts and all. That the Church has covered its eyes perhaps is a hint that it fears such honesty. In admitting to their doubts and weakness, the members of U2 got condemned from the very place where everyone should have raised their hands and said, "Hey, this is a perfect description of my yet imperfect faith. I believe all this, but man, I need to keep running."

As well as another proclaiming of the band's beliefs, this was no doubt a loosening of the dogma and narrow lifestyle of U2's early spiritual days. They had left their Shalom bubble and headed out across the world. What they saw and the people they met had given them a whole new perspective. It not only gave them a more realistic picture of the walk of faith, it also gave them a lot more flexibility in what they could write about when they realized they didn't have to be so intense about perfection and precision. As Bono said around the time of *The Joshua Tree*'s release: "I think there was a certain uptightness to the first three albums…At one time, I thought you had to have all the answers if you were going to write a song, so it was embarrassing to make a record that was filled with doubts and questions. Then I began to see that many of the artists who inspired me—Bob Dylan, Patti Smith, Van Morrison, Al Green, Marvin Gaye—had similar feelings of awkwardness and spiritual confusion. I realize now it's okay to say you still haven't found what you're looking for." [3]

This became a theme for the U2 albums that followed. U2's songs became more and more honest about the struggles of personal faith, as well as the confusion that faith suffers from facing the world. In later songs, the theme would be raised in lines such as "*Like faith needs a doubt*" from "Hawkmoon 269," "*The less you know, the more you believe*" from "Last Night on Earth" and "*And though I can't say why, I know I've got to believe*" from "The Playboy Mansion." In these songs, Bono seems to be trying to give a few clues of what faith really is. It hangs around with doubt and lives far from the scientific certainties of the modern world. Maybe post-modernism was a better canvas to throw out the truth of God's interaction with man.

"I Still Haven't Found What I'm Looking For" had followed "With or Without You" to the top of the charts, the latter being voted *Rolling Stone*'s eighth-best single of all time. The previous decade—from Mount Temple to Live Aid and beyond—seems to have led U2 to this moment. The band members had taken the best aspects of their previous four studio albums and put them together, and all their hopes and dreams came true. *The Joshua Tree* varied in its textures from the almost orchestral build of "Where the Streets Have No Name" to the gospel classiness of "I Still Haven't Found What I'm Looking For" to the raging "Bullet the Blue Sky" to the minimalist "Exit." While *The Unforgettable Fire* painted almost so far outside the lines that lines could not be seen, *The Joshua Tree* drew up new lines that were not confining the band's creativity but mysteriously enhancing it. Consistent and articulate in words and instrumentation, the album was almost flawless.

The only boundary of the subject matter of *The Joshua Tree* was

WALK ON

planet earth. But even then transcendent places beyond the space and time of earth are alluded to in "One Tree Hill," "I Still Haven't Found..." and "Where the Streets Have No Name," which seems to be about some hopeful future place. Niall Stokes says, "He could be talking about heaven. Maybe even offering us a glimpse into some kind of private hell." Ethiopia has been cited as the place with no street names. What about Belfast as a geographical and political anchor? In a city where by your name, or the name of your school, or the name of your street you can be defined into either sectarian camp within seconds and judged accordingly, it would be great to be in a place where the streets have no name and everyone is equal. Maybe the best thing about the song is that everyone can claim these streets as his own.

The Joshua Tree is global. North America is constantly under the bright light of interrogation in both "Bullet the Blue Sky" and "In God's Country." The character in "Exit" is an American living in a country where guns and fundamentalist religion are two pre-occupations. "One Tree Hill" was written in New Zealand and has its reference to Maori religious ritual. "Mother of the Disappeared" touches the catastrophe of Pinochet's Argentina. "Bullet the Blue Sky" was Bono and The Edge's response to American foreign policy in El Salvador. The miner's strike in England is the focus of "Red Hill Mining Town." And Bono finds himself around the corner from his childhood home as he deals with the drug problems of Dublin's Ballymun in "Running to Stand Still." The members of U2 were like documentary journalists investigating the world that their faith had been caressing and colliding with as they crossed the globe frequently in their touring and extra-curricular activity. Without doubt, this is a look at the dark from the place of light, the band allowing their faith to shine around their world and draw questions and conclusions.

In their first decade, Bono only scratched the surface of the heart in his obsession with the soul. He purposely shifted direction with this album.

— YOU KNOW I BELIEVE IT

"Exit" was as interesting in the spiritual direction of U2's work as "I Still Haven't Found…" This was a band that had been giving alternatives to the sex, drugs and rock 'n' roll rebellion. This was a band that was singing the most uplifting and positive of songs—made even more inspirational by The Edge's trademark guitar. On "Exit," Bono, for the first but certainly not the last time, eyeballed the love and goodness of the Christian faith with the demonic, darker side. This was U2's darkest song to date, as Bono disappears down inside the mind of a psychotic killer who shares Bono's belief in "the hands of love." Now here is a contradiction, one without neat and tidy conclusions. Bill Graham suggests that "only a committed believer could have gotten inside the skull of the protagonist of 'Exit.'" [4] The song communicated the truth about a disturbing reality. There must be questions asked about any Christian world-view that would rather sweep that beneath a theological carpet than wrestle with it. U2 would wrestle with it for years to come.

WALK ON

07

The Joshua Tree sessions were a productive time for U2, and the B-sides on the album's singles could have been an album all by themselves. "Spanish Eyes" became a concert favorite, and "Sweetest Thing" became a number one single in the UK eleven years later when it was remixed for *The Best of 1980-1990* compilation. Another brooding piano piece that is closely related to "With or Without You" but wasn't finished in time for the album was "Luminous Times (Hold on to Love)."

"Luminous Times" has a few crucial lines in otherwise interesting but improvised *The Unforgettable Fire*-style lyrics: "*I love you cause I need to/ Not because I need you/ I love you because I understand/ That God has given me your hand/ Holds me in a tiny fist/ And still I need your kiss.*" Bono has one eye in the heavens and the other firmly on earth. Bono always did say that the guys of U2 had their heads in heaven but their feet in the mud. Bono is held in the security of God's love, but still he finds his insecurities throwing him onto the dependence on his wife Ali's kiss.

Bono's relationship with Ali has been an absolute rock in his journey both personally and artistically. Alison Stewart was a schoolgirl sweetheart whom Bono has been with since he was sixteen and married to since he was twenty-two. In the world of pop music, their relationship is an exceptional success. Bono is the first to acknowledge this is due to Ali's strength of character and spiritual steadiness. She has never been satisfied being the wife of a rock star, nor has she been uncomfortable with that. She has studied for a master's degree. She has founded a charity that helps the children of Chernobyl. She is known as a human being of some renown in her own right in Ireland, and she has brought up the couple's four children.

When it came to love songs, U2 was a slow starter. It wasn't until the band's third album that its first clearly defined love songs appeared. Bono had written "Two Hearts Beat as One" in August 1982 about his marriage. *The Unforgettable Fire* touched on their love and domesticity on "Promenade." But *The Joshua Tree* is where U2 really began to look into the romantic heart with the song "With or Without You." Adam told *Rolling Stone*: "The thing is to challenge the radio. To get 'With or Without You' on the radio is pretty good. You don't expect to hear it there. Maybe in church." [5]

Even "With or Without You" is not a plain-sailing love song. There are moments when it appears that it is focusing on the old cliché, "women—you can't live with them; you can't live without them." But then the lyrics twist and turn and deal with a whole lot more than a relationship between men and women. Weaving two or three themes into one song has been another trait of U2's lyric-writing. Niall Stokes, in his song-by-song account of the band's entire catalog, is accurate when he sees erotic love and agape love mixing around here, and also another great U2 theme of surrendering the ego in the lyrics "*give yourself away*" (Luke 9:24). Of course, a person does give himself away in love and marriage, but this kind of surrender could be spiritual or even in opening up to hundreds of thousands of fans every night.

This new discovery of the love song developed even more in *Achtung Baby*, the group's first album of the nineties. In their first decade, Bono only scratched the surface of the heart in his obsession with the soul, and he purposely shifted direction with this album. Bono has commented often that U2 did everything the wrong way around. Other bands started singing about girls and then found the issues of the cosmos and started singing about God; U2 started out singing about God and eventually ended up doing a love album. It wasn't until after all twelve years and six albums that Bono stepped up to a mic and used words such as "baby" and "sugar."

Bono has always held his women, at least his mother and wife, on a pedestal. He told Niall Stokes, "I do tend to idealize women." [6] This is a result no doubt of having lost his mother at fourteen years old. This leaves her, whose face he says he cannot remember, as a bit of a legend. It was a turning point in his life that certainly sent him off seeking God for some solace and direction. "I Will Follow" on the first album is another mingling and interweaving of his fascination with the loss of his mother and his discovery of God. Later on *Pop*, "Mofo" would weave the two again. Not long after his mother passed away and around the same time he ran into God, Bono fell in love with Ali. The fact that Ali is who she is would leave anyone seeing the wonder in womankind. In "Ultra Violet (Light My Way)," Bono sings: "*Oh sugar, don't you cry/ Oh child, wipe the tears from your eyes/ You know I need you to be strong/ And the day is as dark as the night is long/ Feel like trash, you make me feel clean/ I'm in the black, can't see or be seen/ Baby light my way.*" Bono is asking that Ali would be a path for his feet. In many ways, Ali has always been just that.

Bob Dylan's *Blood on the Tracks* is the quintessential heartbreak album. He wrote it coming out of a time of separation from his wife, Sara, and it was the delicate chiseling of beauty out of pain. *Achtung Baby* is U2's version of the same kind of album, less delicate maybe but just as painful and poignant. Heartache is the overriding theme. The songs seem to have their origin in two sources: First, the love that Bono and Ali have and that Bono cherishes. He is aware of her as a spiritual guru filling the gap left by no church connection and being a sense of reality in a rock world where it is easy to lose all perspective on who you are and what life is all about. The other case study is the sadder one. The Edge had married Aislinn O'Sullivan about the same time Bono and Ali wed. The Edge and his wife, too, had a young family but went through a separation that ended in divorce. This is one of the few hiccups in the scandal-free lives of U2's members. Even then, the quiet way the divorce was dealt with is a radical alternative to the tabloid soap operas of most celebrities' love lives.

Bono believed in the miracle of love and has never seemed to doubt that the God dimension is vital to keeping it together. He deals with this sticking together on *Pop*'s "Do You Feel Loved." The song goes: "*Love's a bully pushing and shoving/ In the belly of a woman/ Heavy rhythm taking over/ To stick together/ Man and woman/ Stick together/ Man and woman/ Stick together...*" On "Staring at the Sun," he seems pretty sure where the miracle of the sticking together comes from: "*Over me and you/ Stuck together with God's glue/ It's going to get stickier too.*"

HEARTLAND

U2 has always had a good relationship with America. The band's first gig on the soil of the Promised Land was at New York City's The Ritz in December 1980. Unlike so many bands before them, U2 didn't wait until they broke through in Britain before cracking the U.S. America has loved U2 since the beginning, and the band has been wrapped up in the country even more. When Anthony DeCurtis came to review *Rattle and Hum* at the end of 1988, he confirmed this: "Recorded almost entirely in the United States, the album also carries forward U2's near obsession with the brave new world of America." [1]

Often, Irish kids look to America rather than Britain for their inspiration. Dublin in 1977 had a very different culture than American cities, but the city was exposed to heavy doses of America daily on its televisions. If you are into music, then you are constantly gazing across the Atlantic Ocean to the place your influence comes from. It becomes a mythological land and always leaves you wondering. Sun and big skies and deserts and skyscrapers and those big, big cars. It may be that unless you get in a car on a California highway with the top down and the radio turned up, you will never fully understand rock 'n' roll.

Then there is the other side of the connection. There are more Irish people living in America than in Ireland. As the result of the mass exodus from Ireland to America at the time of the famine and ever since, there are millions upon millions of Americans who claim Irish ancestry. St. Patrick's Day parades are taken more seriously in New York than in Ireland. There is a strong affinity between the two nations. As Bono would say in the song "New York," "*The Irish have been coming here for years/ Think they own the place.*" Maybe it was that Irish-American thing in the back of his mind, but America always had a magnetism for U2.

As the members of U2 set out on tour after Live Aid in support of *The Unforgettable Fire*, they were getting more and more drawn into the American dream and its landscape and nightmare. They were starting to read lots of American writers. Ginsberg, Burroughs, Kerouac and the beat poets must have been intriguing for a band that was on the road so much. Bono would later say, "Allen sort of turned us onto the road, and he broke me into America." [2] He also credits Ginsberg with getting him into the poetry of the Bible: "*Howl* was the one that turned me on because of its biblical roots and discovering how, in the Psalms, ideas rhyme rather than words. The Bible became poetic to me again after reading Ginsberg." Flannery O'Connor also must be seen as one of the influences on a song like "Exit," with its twist and tragic end to religious experience and deepest darkness related to light.

As with "Exit," there was a lot of America on *The Joshua Tree*, including "God's Country" with its crooked crosses and Statue of Liberty coming to rescue the immigrant. It was a big, mysterious, barren American desert on the album's cover. Twelve years later, the band would throw out a phrase that would echo back to the image when in "Mofo" on *Pop* they would be "*looking in the places where no flowers grow*" to find something to save their souls. They were seeking meaning and hope in the desert-scapes.

But if the members of U2 have a lot of questions about the American dream, and even more angry opinions about her foreign policy as in "Bullet the Blue Sky" and "Mothers of the Disappeared," there was still enough fascination and love to go in search of their rock 'n' roll roots. *Rattle and Hum* was a study, a thesis almost, of all the influences of rock 'n' roll. In 1983, the band released its first live album, and it seems Paul McGuinness probably thought it would be a good consolidation idea to do another live album and video. Live albums have been the object of more and more suspicion in recent years, but in the seventies and eighties, they were a way to gain a little time for the band between albums and make a cheap buck from an album that is inexpensive to record. Of course, U2 was not so keen to do something as mercenary or artistically freewheeling as that. On *Rattle and Hum* the band members stretched themselves again. They not only wrote and recorded new songs, but they made a movie that followed a journey through America on tour as well as in a historical search for their influences. Interestingly, when they looked deep into their influences, it was not traveling down the west coast of Ireland to find fiddlers and pipers and the sean-nós (unaccompanied Gaelic Irish singers). It was in America.

WALK ON

Though the Beatles' influence on the band gets recognized in the raucous version of "Helter Skelter," even the reason for its inclu-

> "Dream up the kind of world you want to live in. Dream out loud at high volume. That's what we do for a living."
>
> — HEARTLAND

sion on *Rattle and Hum* had origins in the United States. The reason was to steal the song back from the notorious American murderer Charles Manson, who had used a lot of the lyrics off the Beatles' *White Album*, including lyrics from "Helter Skelter," as prophecy from God that he should indulge in wanton killings. When U2 trawled through its musical heritage, there was Billie Holliday, that "Angel of Harlem" whose jazzy gospel soul singing lit up the forties, and B.B. King, whose blues has stretched out more than half the century. Then there were Dylan and Jimi Hendrix in abundance—Hendrix's version of "The Star-Spangled Banner" and the Dylan song that Hendrix made famous, "All Along the Watchtower." His Bobness himself appeared as a co-writer for "Love Rescue Me." There were also name checks to Miles Davis and John Coltrane. There were delta suns, deserts and ghost ranch hills. There was a "preacher in a traveling show," a spiritual entrepreneur, the likes of whom is rarely found in the Republic of Ireland. There were death rows, skid rows and gangs.

In the movie, there were journeys to Sun Studios and Graceland, and it is a wonder that "Can't Help Falling in Love" came along some years later and not somewhere on the four sides of the vinyl version of *Rattle and Hum*.

The movie and the album have never been seen as a highlight in U2's career. Written off as self-indulgence, they no doubt suffer from being sandwiched between two classics, *The Joshua Tree* and *Achtung Baby*. They were not without merits, though, and the movie had people standing on their seats applauding back home in Dublin as though they had been to a concert. The album did more than simply regurgitate U2 live favorites, though. Similar to what Neil Young had done on *Time Fades Away* in 1973 and Jackson Browne had done on *Running on Empty* in 1977, the stage and places along the road were used as the setting to release new material. The live stuff is emotionally powerful, especially on "Sunday Bloody Sunday," captured on the day of the Enniskillen bombing, and "Bullet the Blue Sky." "Silver and Gold" from the *Sun City: Artists United Against Apartheid* album recorded with Little Steven gets a rockier outing with Bono ordering The Edge to play the blues, which he does in a way that makes it the song's definitive version. The album has at least nine new songs that, maybe apart from "Van Diemen's Land," all stand unembarrassed in the U2 song lists. U2 continued to feature "Love Comes to Town," "Angel of Harlem," "All I Want Is You" and "Desire," the band's first UK number one song, in its live set right up to Popmart, and "Hawkmoon 269" has been described as one of U2's finest moments.

In a quick panorama across the spiritual landscape of *Rattle and Hum*, there is much to cause the listener to stop and ponder.

WALK ON

08

Jesus is called upon for some relief in "Silver and Gold." Again, the cohabitation of good and evil in the same home is disturbingly pointed out in the line *"praying hands hold me down"*— an indictment on the use of the Christian faith to excuse the atrocities against the black majority in South Africa and many other places across the world.

The first rays of lamenting Psalms dawn on *Rattle and Hum,* too. Bono's line *"salvation in the blues"* in "Angel of Harlem" is a reference to what Bono would come back to again and again: that the Psalms were the blues. Then, of course, there is "Love Rescue Me," where he and Bob Dylan revisit Psalm 23 in the lamenting way that U2 would return to throughout the nineties. In some ways, it's a follow-up song to one of Dylan's greatest moments: "Every Grain of Sand," a wonderfully tender and vulnerable testimony of spiritual frailty. "Love Rescue Me" is about a similar spiritual struggler who sees dark shades and reflections and is losing his ability to believe that there is any comfort in King David's rod and staff (Ps. 23:4). But there is still a dim, flickering belief that love will come to bring salvation in the end.

The love that Bono and Dylan are crying out to rescue them is defined in the blues song on the album that delivers that salvation. The love in "Love Comes to Town," written for the great bluesman B.B. King, is clearly the cross of Jesus. "Love Comes to Town" evokes the old gospel hymn when the song says: *"I was there when they crucified my Lord/ I held the scabbard as the soldier drew the sword/ I threw the dice when they pierced his side/ Saw love conquer the great divide."* Again, it is a spelled out proclamation, this time Bono seeing himself as having put his Lord on the cross like the centurion who stood guard at Christ's crucifixion and suddenly realized He was the Son of God. Here, as in "I Still Haven't Found What I'm Looking For," which was given a black gospel remake in the *Rattle and Hum* movie, there is a pointing toward the atonement—"*I saw love conquer the great divide.*"

Love here obviously is made flesh in Jesus, and it is that love that the band claims to believe in on "God Part 2." On this track, the band takes up a dialogue of sorts with its hero, John Lennon, and is happy to stand up for its faith by disagreeing with his 1970 conclusions of who God was or was not. Lennon's song "God" appeared on his *Plastic Ono Band* album, where he railed off a long list of things that he no longer believed in, including The Beatles, Elvis and Jesus. "*God,*" he exorcised, "*was a concept to measure your pain*"—pain being his obsession at the time, having just gone through Primal Scream therapy. "*The dream is over,*" he depressingly announced, and all he now believed in was "*Yoko and me/ That's reality.*" U2's "God," labeled "Part 2," took a more positive angle on belief. Though it also listed what not to believe in, it was much more constructive in its negatives. The list included Uzis, excess, riches, drugs and sexual abuse. The ultimate item, though, was in the opening line: "*I don't believe the devil, I don't believe his lies.*"

It is a behavioral manifesto. This is a clear code of biblical living. It is close to being a sermon against the world's vices that the Kingdom of God opposes. In the end, there is more fighting talk against the devil and his rule across the world: "*I heard a singer on the radio late last night/ Says he's gonna kick at the darkness/ Til it bleeds daylight.*" What a wonderful motto for the Kingdom builder. The lines come from a song by Canadian singzer Bruce Cockburn called "Lovers in a Dangerous Time" from his album *Stealing Fire*.

WALK ON

08

It is hardly likely that the band heard it on the radio. For thirty years, Cockburn has been releasing exquisite albums and never received the recognition he is due. He does have a rabid little following, though, as a result of his virtuoso guitar playing and the poeticism of his lyrics, which like U2 have dealt mainly with spirituality, politics and justice. He has a Christian faith and, again like U2, avoided the ghettos. It is hard to imagine that U2 came across him any other way than because he was a fellow pilgrim. Bono's friend T-Bone Burnett, who later produced some of Cockburn's albums, would no doubt have moved in his circle, and he probably is the link. They also visited South America with the same Christian-based relief agency, though not at the same time, and wrote similarly angry songs about the experience. U2 has even gone on record as saying the band recorded Cockburn's "If I Had a Rocket Launcher," but as U2 couldn't beat his version, it remained unreleased. They did meet in August 1987 when Bono went to the Greenbelt Arts Festival in England just to see Cockburn perform. They spent that night in a hotel room with two of the festival's seminar speakers, John Smith and Gustavo Paragon. Such moments have been U2's church for some years. Interactions with stimulating Christian leaders worldwide in more informal settings have kept U2 members sharp in their Christian worldview.

Maybe the most memorable line on *Rattle and Hum* is not sung but shouted by Bono in the middle of the band's impromptu version of Dylan's "All Along the Watchtower," which they cobbled together, seeking anyone in their road crew who knew the words to enlighten them as they sang in the downtown business district of San Francisco. Bono cries, "All I have is a red guitar, three chords and the truth." Again misconstrued as an egotistical rant, it was another humble cry that these guys had little to offer even musically but they were trying to make something of their privileged position by being honest and seeking some truth in a world full of fraud and anything goes.

"All I have is a red guitar, three chords and the truth."

HEARTLAND

The Love Comes to Town tour that followed *Rattle and Hum*'s release took U2 to the end of what was in many ways its decade. It culminated where it all began, in Dublin, Ireland, with four sell-out nights at the Point Theatre. The New Year's Eve gig was relayed live on radio across Europe. Listeners were encouraged to tape it, and several magazines, including *Hot Press* and *Q*, printed a cut-out cover to put inside cassette boxes. The end of the decade live on the radio was too good an opportunity for Bono Vox to miss. So as midnight approached and a few bars of "Auld Lang Syne" were played, he made the speech that not only raised the emotions of the moment but put a stop to another phase of the band, opening up a door to the nineties. Bono said: "Here she comes: the future. Forget about the past. We're gonna celebrate the future…Seeing as it's New Year's Day, you probably expect me to get all sentimental, yeah? Well, you're exactly right.

WALK ON

Here's to the future! The only limitations are the limits of our imagination. Dream up the kind of world you want to live in. Dream out loud at high volume. That's what we do for a living."

This was a wonderful comment on what was a fulcrum moment in U2's history, a throwaway line in the heat of a heightened adrenalin buzz that could be a thread between the serious political stances of the eighties and what was about to be dreamed up in the nineties. But that wasn't all. This line is full of a preacher's prophetic intent. If anything was to come of any of U2's passionate concerns in the eighties, their audience and those to whom they campaigned would need wild imagination to dream up the kind of world that U2 had come to visualize from their Kingdom of God perspective.

Imagine a world where the blacks in South Africa could learn to forgive and live alongside their white oppressors. Imagine a white government in Pretoria that could see a new South Africa with, by some kind of miracle, Nelson Mandela as president. Imagine that there could be a ceasefire in Northern Ireland where the paramilitaries would lay down their weapons and sit together in a new Northern Ireland government. Imagine if enemies could be loved (Luke 6:27). Imagine if the poor could be fed (Matt. 5:5). Imagine if the meek could inherit the earth. Imagine a world where the first would be last and the last would be first (Luke 13:30). Imagine. Without the turbo-charged engine of imagination, nothing can change in our world. God told his people that they would dream dreams and see visions (Joel 2:28f). Imagining another world and how it could be and how it could work and where to begin to put it together is where the Kingdom begins.

At the end of the eighties, Bono and U2 beseeched their faithful audience to imbibe their passions and dreams and to dream out loud. They would repeat that phrase again as they did their artistic dreaming and imagining in a whole new concept of U2 that would soon be born.

REINVENTION

The video footage conjures up an eastern European mood in the drabbest, greyest and most ominous way. Every shot is close up. Bono is in shiny black leather. There's an onslaught of sound. The Edge's guitar sputters and stutters and shudders onto a different avenue of his trademark minimalism. It's a new, strange incarnation of the familiar. It's almost like he turned down the brightness of the echo effects unit and threw shades of darkness across the U2 horizon. Then there's Bono, his distorted voice heavy, breathing, mumbling out confusion and doubt. Stars are falling, and there are liars and thieves and all sorts of characters struggling to survive in a world as harsh as the new industrial sound.

"The Fly," U2's first single of the nineties, made some of the band's fans shudder. U2 singles have never been predictable. Starting with "Desire" and through the video singles "Numb," "Discothèque" and "Beautiful Day," U2 tends to make its first single from a new album a wake-up call to the radio-listening and video-watching public. "The Fly" was the statement that an album with "Achtung" in its title should make. This band takes great pleasure in pushing its audience to the boundary with the first single. Then, after weeks of uncertainty and doubt, the fans are reacclimated.

A few weeks later, when *Achtung Baby* was released, what the fans would hear on the next track would continue the discomfort. "Zoo Station" came over all industrial, with The Edge giving this funky "grinding of the girders" riff, Bono singing distortedly and the whole thing seeming to be out of sorts, disturbed, turbulent and disconcerting. Bono called for attention: "*I am ready for the laughing gas/ I'm ready for what's next.*" The one certainty was that what's next was going to be very different from what had been. When Bono told the Point Theatre audience two years earlier that the band was going away for a while to dream it all up again, no one could have expected this. Not even U2.

It was a remarkable reinvention. As *Rattle and Hum* looked back to the past in an attempt to discover the roots of what U2 had become, *Achtung Baby* sent the band hurtling into the future. U2 hit the road of the nineties heading even faster than the historical changes in Eastern Europe. It may be the band's best work, eclipsing even *The Joshua Tree* in songwriting, performance and vocals. The photographs and videos revealed Bono behind shades and dressed in hedonistic shiny leather. There were belly-dancers and cross-dressing, and television screens with weird and wonderful slogans. There was even a naked picture of Adam on the cover. There are more songs about love on *Achtung Baby* than the band had ever written before.

Why? What had happened? Had the U2 camp finally broken its ties with Christianity and headed out into the modern world? Here is an album of songs full of irony and lust and betrayal and almost sleaze that seemed to indicate a band that had strayed to the edge of lewd sexuality, just leering over the precipice into a hedonistic abyss. Surely there could be no explanation to this one. The video released a year later has a lot of historical footage and snippets of band interviews. On it, The Edge said, "There are a lot of people a bit puzzled, to be honest, about what we are up to and what we are trying to do."

Certainly, this is true of those within the Church. U2 has suffered at the hands of the great Christian art theft. The band has been misunderstood and maligned and judged for what it does, in many cases because the Church has little desire or ability to understand the arts and is rarely given help from within to look critically at the arts. The robbery has meant that for the vast part of four hundred years, Christians have not thought artistically and have not encouraged the creative among them to develop their gifts. As U2 moved from being a polemic chanting band to an impressionistic and later a persona-wearing, ironic cultural prophet, it largely fell on the deaf ears of the robbed.

North Belfast is a place of division and community tension. There exists the most concentrated microcosm of what has become known as the Northern Ireland troubles. There is a "peace wall," which is actually quite the opposite, that divides the Roman Catholic nationalists from their Protestant loyalist neighbors, literally a stone's throw away. In such an environment, many of the area's youth workers are involved in reconciliation programs, creating safe ways for the youth of both communities to interact, listen, learn and hopefully come to understand one another's religion, political conditioning and culture. In one such program, a youth worker was showing a group of Roman Catholic youth around a Protestant church. As the group came through the building and into the main sanctuary, a startled Roman Catholic boy shouted, "You've been robbed!" Compared to a Catholic chapel, with its statues and icons and multiplicity of artistic representations, the basic, empty, dull, drab Presbyterian building was quite a culture shock.

On the other side of the cosmos, on the other side of time, God moved across the chaos and began to imagine. Colors—blue and green and red and yellow. All the colors somehow mixed together. What would green look like alongside blue, with a little thin band of gold to join the two? Mountains. Oceans. Beaches. Rivers. Trees. Canyons. Valleys. Shapes and textures and smells and taste. All these things existed in God's imagination, even before He decided to make them into a reality and create His artistic masterpiece—the world. God was a Creator (Gen. 1:1). The first thing we learn about Him in the Scriptures is that He was an artist. When we read that man was created in God's image, the only thing we know about God is that He was an artist (Gen. 1:26).

That should have a deep impact on how those who claim to believe and worship and follow His ways work out their salvation and bring in His kingdom in these dawning moments of the 21st century. Yet that young man in north Belfast may have uttered more than a humorous squeal of naive surprise. Maybe he was speaking in prophetic terms. The Church has been robbed. Robbed of art. Robbed of the creative image of God.

Who has robbed the Church? How did it happen? The Church
has robbed itself, and many well-meaning worldviews and ide-
ologies down through the centuries have been the tools that
were used.

The Reformation robbed us of art. When Martin Luther discovered that he could be justified before a holy God by God's grace
and the work of Christ (Rom. 3:21-26), it was a crucial moment
in Church history. In the ensuing division within Roman
Catholicism, many decisions were made in the early days of
Protestantism that were taken as being in reaction to withdrawal
from Catholicism. With many good reasons at the time, the
Reformers reacted to the statues of saints that sometimes
replaced God as the focus of people's prayers. To rid churches of
any art seems to have been a rather imbalanced response. The
Reformers were quick to quote the second of the Ten
Commandments, in which God tells His people, "You shall not
make for yourself an idol in the form of anything in heaven or
on the earth beneath or in the waters below. You shall not bow
down to them or worship them…" (Exod. 20:4). The commandment, though, does not forbid art in church. Eleven chapters
after the commandments, we find that the first person in the
Bible to be described as being filled with the spirit of God is
Bezalel, whom God has given "skill, ability and knowledge of all
kinds of crafts" (Exod. 31:1-11). And he is to use these divinely
given gifts to decorate the Holy Place of worship. Today most
meeting places for worship do not evoke in people the creative
heart of God. People are more likely to think churches have been
robbed. The arts are peripheral.

Modernity also has taken its toll on all things artistic. In the past ten years, there has been an amazing amount said about post-modernity, and there have been evangelicals warning against it as a dangerous new worldview. Any of the lenses by which the world is assessed have to be critically studied, their weaknesses pointed out. For Christians, all worldviews taint definitions of belief and need to be stringently critiqued. Holding post-modernity up to the light of modernity as its winnowing sieve is giving an authority to modernity that is dangerous, but seemingly natural within the evangelical world. Modernity itself is a faulty worldview. It is the failure of modernity in fulfilling its great promises of a better world that has led to its demise.

Under the influence of modernity, the Church became obsessed by definitions and seamless doctrine. Modernity was based on a scientific and rational reasoning that everything could be proven by human experimentation and that this exploration of the scientific field could come up with a superior world and a greatly improved human being. In many ways, this worldview was seen as a huge threat to the mystery of faith. Modernism was driving out the mysteries and belief in a supernatural unseen world, one that was being replaced by a world that could be explained in clear scientific terms. That Christianity should be taken captive by such a system of thought seems a little incongruous, but it led to a couple of centuries of clear systematic theology, apologetics and an overemphasis on the word spoken and written in the communication of Christian truth. Most of these things in themselves are great aids to Christianity's case in the world, but the loss of mystery, experience and any artistic representation of the Gospel was detrimental.

The Bible uses a wide array of creative ways to communicate

truth: law, history, poems, songs, literature, lament, prophesy, proverbs, dreams, angels, miracles, parables, preaching, epistles

> "There are a lot of people a bit puzzled, to be honest, about what we are up to and what we are trying to do."
>
> REINVENTION

and visions. When the evangelicals of the world decided that the Word preached was God's most efficient way of communicating, they overlooked the fact that when Jesus was born, God was saying, among other things, that those ways were not sufficient and that the Word had to become flesh (John 1:1, 14). God's Word is much more than words. Modernity coerced Christianity into taking the flesh and making it into words again. Art suffered. It was not a clearly defined and conclusive kind of rationalism. It left feelings hanging. Stories or songs might stress some points of theological truth and fail to cover other aspects of the Gospel. They missed the fact that Jesus left the crucial doctrine of atonement out of the Parable of the prodigal son (Luke 15:11-32). Jesus, in fact, was much more an artist than a preacher, preferring stories to open the truth and in sometimes oblique ways promising the disciples that those with ears to hear would hear. It could be said that the only writer in the Scripture with any interest in theological definition is the apostle Paul, and though we thank

God for him and the theological explanation of his letters, we must never lose the balance between this and art.

The Puritans also left a negative legacy on art. Though they were sincere in their attempts to lead their followers into good biblical behavioral patterns, there were side effects. There was a tendency to set up boundaries to help progress toward holiness, but that quickly slipped into a judgmental legalism. The general premise to stay safe from any dangers of "the world" led them into an almost dualist approach to the "spiritual" and the "worldly." Art had a tendency to fall into the worldly camp. The Protestant work ethic, which also seems to have its roots in the Puritan legacy, pushed the arts to the fringes. H.R. Rookmaker, in his influential book *Modern Art and the Death of a Culture*, writes, "We can only conclude that the Calvinistic and Puritan movement (at least from the seventeenth century on) had virtually no appreciation for the fine arts, due to a mystic influence that held that the arts were in themselves worldly, unholy and that a Christian should not participate in them." [1]

So what had caused the shift within the U2 camp to this new image on *Achtung Baby*? For some time, it seems the members of U2 had been a little uncomfortable with touring. It had become a job. They had been on the treadmill of the circus that followed the release and phenomenal success of *The Joshua Tree*. There was a feeling in the ranks that they could not go on like this. There was little evidence of this in their high-spirited live performances throughout those three years, but it had taken its toll. They needed to change something.

Then there was fame. The dreams of fame and the hard work

that gets people there never really prepare them for it. Since the beginning, Bono and Adam had believed with little doubt that the spark of U2 was destined to take them to the top. Now that they were at the pinnacle of their field, they discovered the dilemmas and struggles of being the biggest act in rock. Bono was feeling that he was losing who he was in the madness of being a rock star. Lines around his sense of identity were blurring. Being the spokesman for a generation and being constantly out there exposing his beliefs and causes and fighting for this and that had taken its toll. The press had begun to see him as much too serious, and after a decade, the press was beginning to turn. He felt he needed to step back. How could that be done? How about putting on a pair of shades and stepping into a character like the Fly? Personas and play acting would bring with it some protection.

Critically, *Rattle and Hum* had been seen as a bit of a pretentious overindulgence. Critics felt that the band members had gotten a little carried away and were not just tapping into their roots in singing Dylan and Beatles songs and bringing B.B. King on stage and singing about Billie Holliday, but were setting themselves up as their equals. That the band constantly admitted to its failings, on and off vinyl, seems to have been missed. There is no doubt, though, that these guys felt they were becoming caricatures and needed to change the whole darn thing. To go from the critics' caricatures to their own, imagined cartoon personas was the new strategy.

Then there was the challenge. U2 had been assured of its place in the high echelons of rock, but the band members had never made that their goal. That was something that came with their

WALK ON

09

art. Nor was money the most important issue. While most bands set out to get famous, get laid and get rich, these were not the goals of the Christian-hearted U2. The band members were obsessed about something different: their art. Being good at what they did. Becoming better at what they did. Stretching their abilities as far as possible. By the end of the *Rattle and Hum* tour, they were ready to see where they could take it. They needed to spark their imaginations all over again.

How could they do it? Where would they go in their imagination to come up with a reinvention? There had been clues for some time. These clues were hard to see in foresight, maybe even by the band members themselves. But looking back, "Desire" seems to be a major transitional song. It is heading toward the sexual language of *Achtung Baby*, and the "preacher stealing hearts at a traveling show" would be a character that the band would spend some time irrigating and bringing to fruition. "God Part 2" was almost a confession of the weaknesses of *Rattle and Hum*: "*I don't believe in the sixties in the golden age of pop/ You glorify the past when the future dries up.*" It was a huge hint that U2 needed a new source of inspiration. "*I don't believe that rock 'n' roll can really change the world*" is another window into an album that left those high ideals and issue-based songs behind.

It also was becoming obvious in interviews that the boys were at the end of one rich vein. The seam was becoming used up, and a new mine needed to be dug. Bono openly discussed his frustration with being himself when he said: "I don't have an ironic persona like David Byrne or David Bowie to stand behind. It's me up there on the screen, and it makes me cringe." [2]

The scary truth is that when the band members got together in Berlin to crack the top of the new mine and see if the seam was as rich as before, they had little idea what was there. It seems that excavation was a rather difficult job, and it took some time to strike anything at all. At times, they even wondered if the game was over. There had been rumors after the Point Theatre gigs when Bono said it was the end of the road for U2 that maybe he meant it. In the Hansa studios, people wondered if he had been prophetic. That U2 persevered and came out with something as essential as *Achtung Baby* must have at least fulfilled the band's artistic needs.

A year off before the *Achtung* sessions started gave the band time to read and think and be influenced by conversations in the vacuum of commercial or work pressures. The band always has had an artistic, loyal and long-standing inner circle, and in those down times, the members' hanging out and dialoguing and debating constantly threw out ideas. When the guys were wrestling with the need to divide their public and private lives and also to dream it up all over again, their old friend Gavin Friday was in on the conversation. Both Bill Flanagan [3] and B.P. Fallon [4], whose books on the band describe this phase wonderfully, suggest that Friday is in on all the band's social and artistic dealings. As late as *Pop*, he is credited on the album cover as a consultant poptician, and Bono would recognize him and Guggi in interviews post *All That You Can't Leave Behind* as the "no" men in the camp. They are who the U2 guys call when they fear they have lost the plot.

Gavin Friday grew up on the same north Dublin street as Bono. The two have been friends for more than thirty years. Friday has

WALK ON

been a huge influence on the U2 singer. The former Virgin Prune
may have even inspired the entire persona-toting U2. Friday's Prunes

> "I don't have an ironic persona like David Byrne or David Bowie to stand behind. It's me up there on the screen, and it makes me cringe."
>
> REINVENTION

were a performance art band that Bono said was twenty years ahead
of its time. Why these two guys didn't form a band together way
back when is a mystery, apart from the fact, of course, that Bono
answered Larry's ad on the school notice board and hooked up first
with the band that would change the world. Friday started the
Prunes, a Lypton Village gaggle, with Guggi, another lifelong
friend of Bono's.

The Prunes were wild on and off stage, and it would seem that
Gavin was first to leave the Shalom community. Just as he had
been another voice back in the days of the dilemma with rock
and faith, so he seems to have continued to be a man of constant friendly and healthy friction, always throwing another
slant. His natural penchant for throwing other slants headed U2
down the persona road. Friday, having long been the thespian
rock star, obviously had been living out of characters for some
time. When Bono looked to find some new angles, of course he

WALK ON

09

might look to a close friend whose work he greatly admired. Friday was a huge Oscar Wilde fan. He even wrote a song around Wilde's words. It's the title track on his 1989 album *Each Man Kills the Thing He Loves*. The song titles and lyrics on that album contain words such as "Tell Tale Heart," "Another Blow on the Bruise" and "Dazzle and Delight." You can sense what U2 might have been listening to before heading off to Berlin.

Bono's friendship with T-Bone Burnett was another constant at the time. Burnett is the tall, lanky American guitarist on Bob Dylan's Rolling Thunder Review tour who had formed The Alpha Band with the other two coverts of that tour, Steven Soles and David Mansfield, before making a highly acclaimed solo EP, *Trap Door*, in 1982. Bono would co-write "Having a Wonderful Time Wish You Were Her" with T-Bone Burnett for that album's fol-low-up, *Behind the Trap Door*, and "Purple Heart" for *The Talking Animals*. Burnett had a habit—particularly on his *Proof Through the Night* album—of writing songs that could be seen as being written to a woman or to America. Similarly, Flanagan has said that *Achtung Baby* is a suite of songs that could be interpreted as referring to women or God.

Certainly that could be said of "Until the End of the World." Some have seen it as another song of betrayal, and that may be the only way to fit it into the rest of the album's songs of sexual politics. But it can only be about one thing: the betrayal of Christ (John 18:2-6). Judas is not someone to whom Christians have given a lot of time. He was Satan incarnate and sold his soul for thirty pieces of silver. If only Judas' story was that simple. Judas and his story were so complex that Bob Dylan had to wonder, "Did Judas Iscariot have God on his side?" [5] It's a mighty question that like so many other things we want to ignore. As always, Bono faced it head on. For him, it seems to have been one of those rich seams he had been trying to tap.

Bono got inside the story. The closeness of the bride and groom was a wonderful image of the return of Christ at the end of the world, and missing too much, if you stop to think, seems to have been a shot across the bows of post-modern culture that U2 would take on. It could also be an ironic dig at those who would get nothing from this album because they wouldn't stop to think. Kissing Jesus and breaking his heart was a bringing to life of the passion story that seems to have lost its flesh and blood and feelings and pain. Judas' emotions after the act is done are a musical moment of genius. No sermon or Easter reflection could quite conjure such a roller coaster insight into this vital event to the redemption of the world. In the end, we are left to wonder. When Judas reaches for the one he tried to destroy, Bono uses the words of the song title—"Until the End of the World"— which intriguingly in the Gospel are said to the disciples as they head out to convert the world (Matt. 28:20). The promise that he had given to his friends of his eternal loyalty is spoken here to Judas. Does the song conclude with his salvation or damnation?

Without doubt, the spark that lit Bono's Gethsemane flame was a book of poems by Irish poet Brendan Kennelly called *The Book of Judas*. [6] When the book and albums appeared around the same time, both men reviewed each other's work. Kennelly's work is quite a tome, eight years of poems, where profanity sits alongside Christ as he looks at the Judas of Gethsemane, the Judas in our culture and the Judas in us all. In his preface, he asks questions like: "Was Judas the fall guy in some sublime design he didn't even begin to understand? What was he trying to prove? Was he a not-so-bright or too-bright politician? A man whose vision of things was being throttled by another, more popular vision? A spirit not confined to the man who bore the name Judas but one more alive and consequential now at the famined, bloated, trivialized, analytical, bomb-menaced, progressive, money-mad, reasonable end of the twentieth century than ever before?" It's obvious how such questions, and the poems that explored them, would have caught Bono's eye. It's biblical. It's contemporary. It's different from what U2 had been doing. It's not something else, though; it's the same thing from a different angle.

Is that not what poets and songwriters should be doing? Let the systematic theologians spell it out. Let the artists throw out thoughts and slants, maybe even slants no one else has thought of. They should give another view of something familiar to help us learn more about it. They should deal with love, life, good, evil, God, the world and faith. Many of the biblical writers were poets more than they were theologians. Poets and prophets ranted and raved, and storytellers wrote great yarns that all had different slants on God and life and faith. Perhaps the poet's absence from the Church for many centuries has left it deprived of much insight.

One of the most telling aspects of *Achtung Baby* may be how it reveals the artistic heart of U2. Whereas many bands are interested primarily in filling their bank accounts and are not too fussed about saying anything in their music, the members of U2 are artists who need something to say. As they set out in the reinvention of 1991, they were probably trying to make a shallow, not serious U2-type work. They probably were thinking, *Let's just rock*. As the recording process gathered momentum, however, what became obvious was that these guys cannot be frivolous. Since they were teenagers and found faith in Christ, they had been asking cosmic questions. It was not going to be possible to back out now.

In some ways, the cover and title were the only funny things about the album. It seems Joe O'Herlihy used the phrase "Achtung Baby" endlessly during the Hansa sessions in Berlin, having picked it up off the Mel Brooks film *The Producers*. It's a title that has been highly criticized as foolish, and Bono felt the press would have been even harder on the band had it not been frivolous in the packaging. He said at the time: "It's a con, in a way. We call it *Achtung Baby*, grinning up our sleeves in the photography. But it's probably the heaviest record we've ever made." [7]

The Edge's divorce was part of the reason for the "blood and guts" on the album. Bono would say, though, that The Edge's struggles at the time were far from the only influence. The songs were about what many of his friends were struggling with at the time. The whole miracle of two people finding love and then the hard work of maintaining it was a universal theme. That the band was recording the album at the end of communism in East Germany, and that the guys were watching the Persian Gulf War between sessions, had to have an effect, even though there is little point of reference to all that in the lyrics apart from "Zoo Station." This song was the gateway to the east or west, depending on which way a person was heading, and that crossroads image was a perfect lead track for a band heading toward its own kind of freedom.

The opening lyrics to "Zoo Station"— *"I'm ready, ready for the laughing gas/ I'm ready, ready for what's next"* —were clearly a sign that this song was simply about the band and the reinvention. What was happening in the band would be tangled up or woven into what was going on in the relationships around Bono, as well as what was going on in his own head, heart and soul. "One," which is the torch song of the album, seems to have evolved around Eno finding two melodies that the band decided to play over each other with Bono ad-libbing as he played them. Hence, *"We are one, but we are not the same."* It then becomes more, but it's a tapestry of Bono's thoughts.

It is inevitable that another intricate part of the tapestry would be his faith. As they couldn't be frivolous if they tried, they couldn't leave God out if they tried, either. As well as in "Until the End of the World," which was written for the Wim Wenders movie of that name, Jesus appears in "One" and in the song of Bono's spiritual hypocrisy, "Acrobat." Following Flanagan's suggestion to hear all U2 love songs as songs to God and see how they change becomes as interesting as ever on *Achtung Baby.* [8] There are those who would see *"she moves in mysterious ways"* as a clear nod at that phrase's original usage for God. In 1993, there would be more echoes of such a thought on Bono and Gavin Friday's title song for the movie *In the Name of the Father,* "*In the name of a father/ And his wife the spirit.*" God as a woman is something that would raise many Christian heckles, but U2 was not the first to use the feminine for God. Jesus used it in the parable of the widow's mite (Luke 15:8-10) or to describe God as a Hen looking after Her chicks (Matt. 23:37), and Isaiah used "mother" as a way to describe how God comforts his people" (Isa. 66:13). To limit God to the male gender would be to make

WALK ON

09

Him something less than God and mean that women are not
made in his image.

The song ends with the female fusing into the spirit: *"Spirit moves
in mysterious ways/ She moved with it/ She moves with it/ Lift my
days and light up my nights."* The song shows that God is there in
the midst of all the struggles, that He sees the man inside the
immature behavior of the child, and that if you're going to reach
for anything in this life, *"you've got to get on your knees."*

EVERYTHING YOU KNOW IS WRONG

As the lights went down, there was a bugle call. The 36 televisions that were scattered across the stage were fuzzy and flickered, seeking to catch some kind of signal. Suddenly, slogans were spilt across the screens in split-second, fit-inducing flashes. TV pictures of sports and politics and science and fashion mingled in a good, bad and ugly of what was post-modern entertainment. The frivolous sat alongside the serious so they blended in to one another. There was a flickaholic in the room, as there now is in every living room across the world, changing channels at a speed that allows no one to get bored, but lets no one get a handle on what's happening. Television screens arrayed the entire stage, and a video wall was drowning out the band. Welcome to Zoo TV.

Dreaming it up all over again had never sounded or looked so true. There had been feverish anticipation as U2 took the stage in Lakeland, Florida, for what would be the first U2 gig in America in almost five years. Those who came looking for news were not disappointed. It is hard years later to remember the impact these first Zoo TV shows had. Here were four former bohemian young men who, in the guise and tradition of the hippy years, had shouted out their causes and slogans in rock 'n' roll music, all glitzed up like a glam rock band or back to the new romantics they had helped rid the world of. It was as if they had left their crusty trailer park and relocated on Wall Street or in Hollywood. There were even hints of Vegas Elvis. It was some transformation. Up until this point, backdrops were about as exciting as U2 stage shows got, maybe with Bono taking hold of a big spotlight and shining it on a feverish Edge guitar solo. That night the band was almost a backdrop or soundtrack to a stage show like never before. It was hard to imagine, but imagination was exactly where it was all born. Bono said at the time, "We've got all this technology available, and it's our duty to abuse it." [1]

Dwarfed by the images flashed in glitzy, fast-moving colors and a noise that could be described as "dreaming out loud" was Bono, in shiny leather and throwing shapes. Acting. Fooling. Mocking. The images continued to flash around him.

EVERYTHING YOU KNOW IS WRONG

ENJOY THE SURFACE

AMBITION BITES THE NAIL OF SUCCESS

BELIEVE EVERYTHING

TASTE IS THE ENEMY OF ART

BELIEVE

WATCH MORE TV

CELEBRITY IS JOY

MOCK THE DEVIL

GUILT IS NOT OF GOD

EVOLUTION IS OVER

ROCK 'N' ROLL IS ENTERTAINMENT

SERVICE IS NOT INCLUDED

IT'S YOUR WORLD—YOU CAN CHANGE IT

Words to confuse and words to depress. Words of truth and words to inspire. Words to slit your wrists to. Words to worship to. Where do you look? What do you believe? The audience's senses were bombarded with stimuli and assaulted by the truth and lies of the word-bites that pummeled them. It was manic and thrilling. It was gripping and overwhelming. For the first few songs of the set, it was hard to focus on any particular thing. Whereas Bono's charisma had been central to U2 gigs for some fourteen years, suddenly he had to compete with the flashing words and brightly colored images. But that was the point. This was a spectacle, not Bono. U2 was in hiding, behind its art form, its technology, its music and the modern world.

It was a post-modern overload of subliminal messages that con-tradicted one another and left the audience screen-shocked and

WALK ON

confused. At the same time, it almost celebrated and denigrated the post-modern world. That, in itself, is what post-modernism is all about. And in some ways, that might be its strength. Evangelical Christianity has been scathing of the onset of post-modernism. It has been seen to be the purveyor of relativism. Zoo TV was not about the answers of truth as much as it was about asking questions about what truth is and using those questions to question what the human race in the western world is all about at the end of the second millennium. Maybe God was not so much answering prayer as He was asking questions that He's already given us all the resources to answer. The members of U2 always have been able to live with the questions of faith and have said they were just asking a different set of questions. They have been able to live with contradictions, too. They have been able to live in the heart of the contradictions to give life to their art and journeys.

Flanagan sees the start of Zoo TV as during the recording of *Achtung Baby* when Bono and The Edge watched the Gulf War live on television. This was the first time you could watch cruise missiles heading down the streets of Baghdad. It was fascinating, gripping and frightening. Entertainment and real-life war was blurring where *"fact is fiction and TV reality."* Flanagan said, "When U2 tours behind this album, they have to figure out a way to represent this new reality." [2] In the midst of the Zoo TV spectacle, there was a lot more happening than just humor and irony and a rock 'n' roll extravaganza to beat all rock 'n' roll extravaganzas. This was as carefully put together as a play on Broadway or in London's West End. Bono's words and postures were scripted, and his personas were to hide behind. But the disguise would allow him to reveal so much more.

When the final outworking of those thoughts while watching the Gulf War became Zoo TV, one has to wonder if Bono in the meantime had been reading Neil Postman's book *Amusing Ourselves to Death*. [3] The premise of this influential 1985 book was: "All public discourse increasingly takes the form of entertainment. Our politics, religion, news, athletics, education and commerce have been transformed into congenial adjuncts of show business largely without protest or even popular notice. The result is that we are a people on the verge of amusing ourselves to death." In his foreword, he looks at the prophecies of George Orwell and Aldous Huxley. Postman says he thinks Huxley got it right when he feared that we would not have truth concealed as Orwell thought, but that truth would become irrelevant in thoughtless, trivial culture.

"Amusing Ourselves to Death" would have been a wonderful strap line for Zoo TV. If Postman had used the very technology he feared to communicate his point, then he would have come up with Zoo TV. What U2 conveyed so powerfully on stage in the early nineties was that we were trivializing life. We were making the absurd normal. Canadian novelist Douglas Coupland, most famous for his books *Life After God* and *Generation X*, has taken on a similar theme in his book *Polaroids From the Dead*. He points out that "soon the planet will be entirely populated by people who have only known a world with TVs and computers." He then asks, "When this point arrives, will we continue with pre-TV notions of identity?" [4] The reality of the unreality of this TV-shaped world was portrayed on Zoo TV.

As part of this play to expose the absurd, Bono took on two personas. The Fly, with his shiny leather suit and shade glasses, is an over-the-top hedonistic rock star. Bono played this character on and off stage. Frivolous, rude and foul-mouthed, he would avoid the serious issues of life, contrary to the serious young Bono Vox from U2. He even removed his clothes during an interview with UK magazine *The Face*. The Fly himself had another persona in the Mirrorball Man. Coming out for the encore to sing "Desire," Bono—dressed in his gold-lamé suit—brought a mirror so he could pose in front of it. In a bizarre twist of fate, or thoughtless critique, this led to Bono being labeled as an egocentric poser. Yet there is nothing so humble as to make fun of yourself and of the position people think makes you important. To stand up and expose the seeming nonsense of it all seems far from egotistical. But many had lost the real Bono beneath the personas. In some ways, that had been the whole point. It was all about ego and raunchy post-modern Elvis sexiness. For many, it was what they had always believed: Bono was full of himself, and they were seeing the real him at last.

In reality, it was one of the absurdities to be exposed. He said at the time that rock music was absurd—"four jerks in a limousine" was his phrase. [5] The band was keen to show the lunacy of what it had been made into. Why should four guys who played guitars and drums and sang a few songs be taken so seriously and put into such positions of power and money and sexual idolatry? That was, pretty much, the theme of the whole shebang—to expose modern culture and let people see the shallow nonsense that it was.

The idea of mocking the world was closely linked with the third persona in Bono's new repertoire. This character threw Christendom even more. McPhisto was a horn-wearing devil, and Bono played the part so well that many within the Church thought he had sold his soul to the opposition. Bono told Joe Jackson a story of how he had encountered a concerned Christian girl who did not understand: "One night I was doing

"It was about world—weariness, which, in a sense, is what U2 is going through."

EVERYTHING YOU KNOW IS WRONG

my Elvis-devil dance on stage with a young girl in Wales, and she said, 'Are you still a believer? If so, what are you doing dressed up as the devil?' I said, 'Have you read *The Screwtape Letters*, a book by C.S. Lewis that a lot of intense Christians are plugged into? They are letters from the devil. That's where I got the whole philosophy of mock-the-devil-and-he-will-flee-from-you.' She said, 'Yes,' and I said, 'So you know what I am doing.' Then she relaxed and said, 'I want to bless you.'" [6] In *The Screwtape Letters*, Lewis sought to expose the cunning plans of the devil so people would be shocked into realizing where they were being duped and lied to and deceived. U2 took on this strategy, too. On the American leg of the Zoo TV tour, Mirrorball Man appeared as something of a shady rock star who could have been a cross between Jerry Lee Lewis and his cousin, Jimmy Swaggert. Mirrorball Man wore a cowboy hat and threw away dollars like

WALK ON

10

confetti. When the tour came to Europe, Bono felt the televange-
list would need a new slant for a different context. Somewhere
along the way, Mirrorball Man metamorphosed into McPhisto,
the place where Satan meets insincere rock star ego. It is all the
worst of what Elvis could have become.

C.S. Lewis' influence on Bono's life and work should be no surprise. Bono has always had a bit of a soft spot for Christian writers. Way back in time, the band would mention Christian writer
Francis Schaeffer in interviews as being a significant influence on
it. In addition, in 1998, Bono chose Eugene Peterson's poetic
paraphrase of the New Testament, *The Message*, as one of his
books of the year. Lewis was born in 1898 in Belfast. He spent
most of his life in Oxford as a lecturer and writer. In literary
terms, he is best known for his wonderful allegorical children's
books *The Narnia Chronicles*, which took Christian thoughts and
made them into wonderful allegories in books that sent children's imaginations racing long before the birth of Harry Potter.
Though Lewis was selling books of apologetics within the
Church, he had a strong desire and sense of vocation to bring
the truth he believed in to a wider market through his fiction.
Here, he had a lot in common with U2.

In an essay called "Sometimes Fairy Stories Say Best What's To Be
Said," Lewis wrote, "I thought I saw how stories of this kind
could steal past a certain inhibition which had paralyzed much
of my own religion in childhood. Why did one find it so hard to
feel as one was told one ought to feel about God or about the
sufferings of Christ? I thought the chief reason was that one was
told one ought to. An obligation to feel can freeze feelings. And
reverence itself did harm. The whole subject was associated with

lowered voices, almost as if it were something medical. But supposing that by casting all these things into an imaginary world, stripping them of their stained-glass and Sunday school associations, one could make them for the first time appear in their real potency? Could one not thus steal past those watchful dragons? I thought one could." [7] That is a succinct appraisal of what U2 was trying to do in Zoo TV.

A few years after the birth of McPhisto, Bono said a character in "The Black Rider," Tom Waits' 1993 theatrical collaboration with William Burroughs and Robert Wilson, inspired McPhisto. The Edge said, "Bono and I saw that show in Hamburg, and I thought there was a certain license in that figure that would be interesting for Bono. It wasn't just Bono. It wasn't the other three members of the band going, 'Oh my God, he's wearing devils horns! How embarrassing!' We were into it." [8] As the character was in the thought-stream, Bono's best buddy, Gavin Friday, suggested the horns. Whether it was at or before that moment, or later in McPhisto's incarnation, somewhere along the line he became a Screwtape.

Around the same time, Joe Jackson interviewed Bono for a book he was writing tentatively called *In Search of Elvis*. Jackson had been aware of the Elvisness of much of Zoo TV, especially the ending where Elvis and McPhisto kind of duet. Bono says: "The whole encore section is kitsch, it's Elvis/ second-hand car salesman/ the devil, before I got into McPhisto. That's what I saw him as: an Elvis-devil. It was about world-weariness, about being in a jaded, fat Elvis period, which—in a sense—is what U2 is going through. But part of it all was 'stardom' and the decadence implicit in that supposed lifestyle. So we began with 'Money,

WALK ON

10

Money, Money,' then 'Desire' and ringing up the president, whatever. It's the derangement of stardom. And we paint that kind of portrait until finally we come through to the soul of that with 'With or Without You' and 'Love Is Blindness'—the repentance." [9]

To U2 and most thoughtful artists, the problem with Christians is the Church has for many years taught people *what* to think and not *how* to think. Everything has to be explained in such lin-

> That was the theme of the whole shebang—to expose modern culture and let people see the shallow nonsense that it was.
>

ear terms. Whether it was that night in Wales, or whatever it was, Bono seems to have thought it important to throw out clues to the rest of the Christians who were not getting it. In the video cartoon for "Hold Me Thrill Me Kiss Me," McPhisto is knocked to the ground by a car, and a book flies out of his hand. The camera follows the book, which hits the ground, and the front of the book says, "*THE SCREWTAPE LETTERS—C.S. LEWIS.*"

The Screwtape Letters begins with two quotes, from Thomas More and Martin Luther. Luther says, "The best way to drive out the devil, if he will not yield to the texts of Scripture, is to jeer and flout him, for he cannot bear scorn." [10] More says: "The devil...the proud spirit...cannot endure to be mocked." So the devil hams it up and tells the audience that he is in control of the world, from politicians to religious leaders, and thanks the audience for making him who he is.

If we just take the Dublin monologue as an example, Bono ends a stage of the Zoo TV tour with this message from McPhisto: "You know who I am. Oh I know who you are. I know you probably even better than you yourself. What a night. What a show. Zooropa. It's all over. So many have turned out to see us, I don't know what to say. Thank you, thank you, thank you...But you know there is someone who used to come and see us all the time and who hasn't been around for a while. We used to be so close. People think I have forgotten about him, but I haven't. I used to find him so inspiring back then. He invented me. I was his most magnificent creation. The brightest star in his sky. Now look at me. A tired old pop star in platform shoes. I try to speak to him all the time, but he won't take my calls. And I get blamed for everything. All the wars, all the famine, all the trouble in the world. I get blamed for it. Even the *Evening Herald* slags me off. Who can I get to make me make peace with him? Who will mediate for me? Shall I call the United Nations? Maybe they could help me. Off with the horns, on with the show..."

It's a marvelous monologue. Bruce Springsteen, of course, was the inventor of the long story in the middle of songs, but here is one man out on a stage in front of thirty thousand people holding them in the palm of his hand without a band suggesting that they would rock back into some hit song at any time. This is a fantastic piece of showmanship, with all kinds of nuances as

Bono slips into his character as the devil and then pop star. From a biblical sketch of who the devil is, he turns into himself being ripped apart by the Dublin press, then almost spelling out what the Christian fraternity thinks, that he has left God behind some- where, then bringing it all to a fervent preacher's final questions: Who will bring us peace with God? Who will mediate for us? That he then brings in his other nightly prop of technology and phones, the United Nations could be seen as a frivolous ending or the most poignant of all endings. Who does mankind trust? C.S. Lewis would have been proud.

11

MIDNIGHT IS WHERE THE DAY BEGINS

The very sound of the title track of *Zooropa* conjures up images of a futuristic European city, at a time just after midnight. *Zooropa* is about what lies beneath the neon lights, the promises of fame and fortune, and the pleasures of the modern world. It's the place where "*midnight is where the day begins*" ("Lemon"), where "*it's cold outside, but it's brightly lit*" ("Zooropa"), where "*man builds a city of banks and cathedrals*" ("Lemon"), where "*the streets are paved with gold*" ("The Wanderer"), where we are still looking at the world through television and cinema screens ("Babyface," "Lemon," "Zooropa"). In some ways, Bono again is giving a bit of a commentary on what U2 is doing. This is so in "Stay (Far Away So Close)," as the band describes Zoo TV: "*Far away, so close/ Up with the static and the radio/ With satellite television/ You can go anywhere/ Miami, New Orleans, London, Belfast and Berlin.*"

In this collection of songs, we are also given a look beneath the surface of this night time, fun time cityscape—and the heart of it all is found wanting. Underneath the streets, paved with gold, the stones are lifted to reveal "*the skin and bones of a city without a soul*" ("The Wanderer"). The things that are being held onto so tightly, "*you've already lost it*" ("Dirty Day"). "*Dressed up like a car crash*" as in "Stay," the victim of this darkness finds her "*wheels are turning, but you're upside down.*" "Numb" is maybe the conclusion of the soulless city. The technology, the promises of the advertising, the bright lights and good looks of the surface of things have you realizing that "*everything is numb and too much is not enough.*"

Achtung Baby and Zoo TV had revived U2's desire to make music. With all the paraphernalia that the Zoo TV world tour brought with it, the band just wanted to make new music. Feeling music-weary after *Rattle and Hum*, the band members' passion was back. The reinvention had re-ignited the old fires. The new angles that they had given themselves were giving their imagination the head of steam needed to keep the U2 journey hurtling on. In 1993, U2 was a band picking up a fresh impetus, having run on momentum alone for far too long.

Literally recorded between the U.S. and European legs of the band's Zoo TV outside broadcast tour, *Zooropa* was originally planned as an EP to keep the inspiration fuse lit, but it turned into an extra album. Bands of U2's stature were not in the habit of releasing two albums in such a short time. Being recorded so quickly during a tour perhaps has caused *Zooropa* to be taken less seriously in the U2 canon. It may not have been seen as a follow-up to *Achtung Baby* as much as a stopgap release. It also lost out in that having been recorded so quickly, there was little room left for maneuver between its completion and the first gig of the tour's next leg. That meant it didn't get the live exposure new albums need to register in the minds of fans. The band just didn't have time to rehearse it. Bono would explain on stage, "Well, it was a fine thing writing some songs and putting out a record while you are still on tour, but it's another thing trying to play the ****** things." As a result, only "Stay," "Lemon" and a version of "Numb," where at times The Edge read the lyrics off a music stand, made it into the set list.

In musical terms as well as in concept, lyric, persona and creative storytelling, *Zooropa* deserves serious consideration. The band members had broken free of their old selves, all the expectations of their eighties caricatures. They had found irony and humor. They had hidden beneath image and new personas. They had paddled in the shallows of investigating and then exposing the post-modern and technological age. Then they had been dragged into the deep whirlpool of it all, where the culture they feared was drowning. As they exposed it to others, more and more they were uncovering the darkness beneath its shiny surface. So when it came to the down time between tours, there was so much to say and too little time in which to say it.

Zooropa is full of complex characters looking at life from a plethora of angles and from a darker perspective than the band was used to. There are those very different, bizarre, almost perverted views on life—and especially faith. The cold and almost wicked way Bono sings "Daddy's Gonna Pay for Your Crashed Car" could almost be a snide attack on the wealthy father who throws money foolishly at his spoiled children. It could be about the devil being someone's sugar daddy. If you sell me your soul, I'll bail you out. Then again, it could be a reworking of the story of the prodigal son.

WALK ON

11

When Jesus told the story of the prodigal son (Luke 15:11-32), it was a scandalous yarn. This boy was a rogue who had lived the wildest end of hedonism and, in the process, blew his dad's hard-earned inheritance. He partied and whored it away. He was irresponsible and lived the model sinner's life. As he was heading back home, the crowd, the Pharisees in particular, were getting ready for the most justified and harshest of judgment. When Jesus stung the tail of the tale with a merciful tenderness, kind-ness and warm-hearted love, the sense of heckles that must have gone up in the hearts of the Pharisees could almost be felt and heard. That Jesus then went on to expose their response in the good son's lack of grace to his brother and abhorrence at his father's grace made it even more outrageous. "Daddy's Gonna Pay for Your Crashed Car" could be Bono trying to invoke a sim-ilar disbelief and outrage. Could grace really be this ridiculous? Could it really be such nonsense that God would let you drive the most reckless of lives, then when you crash, offer another chance? It is scandalous, irrational and revolutionary.

"The First Time" is one song that has topped the conversations of the most discerning of believers. What on earth? Throwing away the keys of the Kingdom and leaving by the back door? Again, many from within the Christian fold saw this as another renouncement of the band's faith—signed, sealed and delivered. One of the misconceptions with any artist is that everything they sing, write or create is subjective and always in the character of the singer, author or artist. At this stage of U2's musical journey, the band had hidden behind characters like the one in "The First Time." Bono was narrating someone else's story.

Niall Stokes' book shows how Bono was playing around with the angles of the camera on the biblical stories. It seems the song had been written for Al Green in the same way that "Daddy's Gonna Pay for Your Crashed Car" apparently was written with

> At this stage of U2's musical journey, the band had hidden behind characters. Bono was narrating someone else's story.
>
> — MIDNIGHT IS WHERE THE DAY BEGINS
MIDNIGHT IS WHERE THE DAY BEGINS

John Lee Hooker in mind, and "Mystery Girl" had been given to Roy Orbison. There was also "Slow Dancing," with Willie Nelson in mind, and "Two Shots of Happy, One Shot of Sad," with Frank Sinatra in mind. Bono said about the Green song: "We decided to keep it for ourselves. Brian really loved it. But instead of doing an 'up' version, we just emptied it out, deconstructed the song and ended on this line about throwing away the key, and the prodigal doesn't go back. He sees all this stuff there for him and he doesn't want it and he goes off again. That's a really interesting take on the story." [1] It sure is. Isn't that what art is all about? Let the theologians fight over how it is. The artists are there to get around the corners of the story, to ask how it might have looked from here or over there, to ask what might have happened if this had happened instead, and what light that might shed on the whole deal.

"The Wanderer" is another almost blasphemous yarn to the puri-

tanical listener. Apparently, Bono had Ecclesiastes in mind for
this conclusion to his own little thesis on the futility of a life
without God. In some ways, *Zooropa* might be U2's version of
what Douglas Coupland was talking about in his book *Life After
God.* [2] The working title to this final track was "The Preacher."
(Eccles. 1:1—the writer of Ecclesiastes in the King James
Authorized Version of the Bible is called "The Preacher.") The
Edge seems to have been the one who suggested "Wanderer" as
an alternative, but a preacher still he is, and in some ways, he
might be the inspiration for the Robert Duval movie *The Apostle.*
As in the Old Testament book of Ecclesiastes, which sits snugly
alongside the work of nineties U2, there is someone searching
for where he might find meaning: "*I went out there/ In search of
experience/ To taste and to touch/ And to feel as much/ As a man can/
Before he repents.*" As an album, *Zooropa* is a wander through
modern culture, and that is where the whole thing concludes.

Bill Flanagan's book *U2 at the End of the World* says there was
debate as to whether Bono should replace Cash as vocalist.
Flanagan says, "I think that the real reason Bono does not want
to sing 'The Wanderer' is because when Bono sings the song, it
comes off as a mea culpa for all the glitz and surface that U2 has
spent the last two years creating. When Bono sings 'The
Wanderer,' it seems like a public confession that beneath the fly
shades, he is hoping to find God by searching through the glitter
and trash." [3] Finding the Divine in the trash is paraphrased in
'Mofo' from *Pop.*

Flanagan's book also speaks of debate between him and the
band about antinomianism. [4] This is a heresy that has the sinner
almost creating and performing as much sin as possible so grace

can abound as much as possible. Around the time *Zooropa* was being recorded, Maria McKee, a friend of U2's, was releasing an album called *You Gotta Sin to Get Saved*. McKee was a Christian who had jumped headlong into the world of rock music with her band Lone Justice. In her late teens, she wooed the rock world with her voice, good looks and Bono-type charismatic stage performance. She also had talked openly about her Christian faith. One of her most successful singles was "I Found Love": *"The beginning and end of every wish/ Is balanced in the center of a vision like this/ Maybe my emotions are inclined/ To surrender to the notion of a glorious kind."* Her musical life could have been weaned on a strict diet of *October* and *War*. Live, she went into a celebratory rant in the middle of "I Found Love" that had her giving an American preacher's ecstatic exclamations of redemption and salvation.

McKee had moved to Dublin at the end of the eighties, drawn by the creative rock music vibe of the city, the tax breaks for artists and her friendship with U2, which had its origins in their shared faith. Maybe Flanagan was onto something when he brought up antinomianism with the band. Maybe it was as much a pastoral discussion as it was a journalistic investigation. Maybe the band members were living too close to the experimental end of their art. Maybe after their sheltered late teens and early twenties, the temptations of the world were beginning to entice them. Maybe as they looked at the dark and the light, the dark was becoming too appealing.

Even if this was true, this band probably has the fewest tabloid gossip-column appearances in the history of rock music. Adam, who lived the most hedonistic life of the four, never taking hold of the whole Christian ethos, was the target of a drug bust in Dublin and missed a concert in Australia as a result of alcohol abuse. He later came clean. That is the sum total of scandal in this band in an industry where the public could be mistaken for thinking sensational headlines were part of the job description. For a Christian to get a little fond of Jack Daniels and openly confess to be enjoying the party life may be some great evangelical scandal, but in the world this band moved in, it was tame, almost boringly good behavior.

. . . UNDER THE TRASH

It was a brief second in the Popmart set. It was a tiny moment
with enormous meaning. It was a throwaway gesture in which
the whole Popmart thesis is understood. Perhaps it was even the
whole point of the U2 dissertation of the nineties. The band was
cranking up the volume in "Mofo" when Bono came to the line
"*Looking for the baby Jesus under the trash.*" As he sang those
words, he gestured his arm to the biggest TV screen in the world,
that huge golden arch and that mighty lemon. It was almost just
a shrug, but the illumination it threw out was as bright as every
spotlight, special effect or image Willie Williams was flashing up
from the light desk. All of this paraphernalia the band had
around it night after night for most of the nineties was trash.
What was more important was underneath it all. The use of Baby
Jesus could mean the genesis of this thought is in the commer-
cialization of Christmas, when Jesus, the real meaning behind
the season, is lost beneath wrapping paper, tinsel, stuffing and
Santa Claus. But it is a picture of a general loss of meaning or

hope or truth. As we glance across the horizon of the loudest and brightest culture in the history of humankind, is there any chance we might find in the midst of all the shallowness something deeper, something more precious, something more lasting? Is Jesus lost? Or can He be retrieved from the garbage?

Pop and Popmart, the next U2 live extravaganza, had much more kitsch, glitz and, well, pop than the Zoo TV and *Zooropa* period. *Pop* was the third album in the trilogy of technology, loops, irony, humor and persona. It did move away from the European underground city sounds of both *Achtung Baby* and *Zooropa*. Musically, there was a nod in the direction of dance music. Scottish hip-hop expert Howie B came on board to keep the band sounding youthful and still involved in the musical technological conversations of the nineties, when bands such as the Chemical Brothers, Massive Attack and Prodigy were becoming major players.

U2 took some time off after *Zooropa*. It was the band's first lengthy break in nearly twenty years. When the members reconvened to look at what they might do next, a lot of fresh ideas were buzzing around. Adam told Robert Hilburn of the *Los Angeles Times*: "I think we needed that break to get away from each other for a while and explore music without worrying about what U2 should be doing...At the end of that period, we started to realize that we were actually all listening to the same music. I was listening to bands called Leftfield, Massive Attack and Underworld. Bono and The Edge were listening to Prodigy and the Chemical Brothers, as well as Oasis and some others." [1] Bono had seen two distinct directions going on around the band members and was interested in what they would add to U2.

Bono said, "We liked the tendency in England toward pop song-writing in the (traditional) way of Lennon-McCartney and Lou Reed—something that Noel Gallagher and Oasis are doing. But we also liked the energy and adventurousness of the techno, hip-hop world. So we decided to explore bringing these two disciplines together. That's what this record is about." [2] It would be wrong to simply pigeon-hole *Pop* as U2's modern dance record. It was experimental and it was a band competing with its peers, but at no stage did it degenerate into any kind of gimmick to be trendy. The album was still U2. No matter how the band members decided to re-dream it, it always sounded like U2.

When U2 went on tour for *Pop*, there was a visual shift of stagescape, too. From a television studio, U2 took its inquisitive investigations to the other great altar of the late twentieth century. It was as if the band had built a stage slap bang in the middle of a shopping mall. In fact, the U2 guys launched the tour at a Kmart. It was back to America, the world's Capitol Hill of capitalism. This time, it was out of the desert and into the malls of the city. Here they were again, setting up their spot to give another exposé of the modern ills. While *Zooropa* looked at fame and power, *Pop* looked at the consumerist dream of progress with its empty philosophy of "I buy tacky products, therefore I am."

It was that searching for Jesus under the trash. "Mofo," which kicked off the shows, begins with that statement of intent: "*Looking for to save my save my soul/ Looking in the places where no flowers grow/ Looking for to fill that God shaped whole.*" Bono is peering out from behind those shades again, and "Mofo," with its nod in the direction of John Lennon's song "Mother," is again Bono in intimately subjective muse as he tries to deal with the

WALK ON

12

death of his mother and how that loss has shaped him through the years. It finds him *"Lookin' for a sound that's going to drown out the world/ Lookin' for the father of my two little girls/ Got the swing, got the sway, got the straw in the lemonade/ Still lookin' for the face I had before the world was made."* There is something of the pop star, the family man and the spiritual pilgrim about that verse. It's as if Bono is crying out to God that in finding those three in balance, he will find that something he needs to fill the God-

> **"I went looking for spirit and found alcohol; I went looking for soul, and I bought some style; I wanted to meet God, but they sold me religion."**
>
> — UNDER THE TRASH

shaped hole. There are still no comfortable refuges in the life of this Dublin boy, but the search continues. The compass points have not changed even though he may be in the wilderness in some kind of Old Testament wandering. It is still that "God-shaped hole" that captures the thinking of his heart, soul and mind.

Further into the Popmart concerts, Bono would shout, "I went looking for spirit and found alcohol; I went looking for soul, and I bought some style; I wanted to meet God, but they sold me religion." U2's latest mission in dadaism was to erect the

WALK ON

12

cathedrals of today's religion, expose its emptiness and then try to dig deep down somewhere for Jesus in the midst of it all. He isn't even as easily found in the places you might expect to find Him, as the song "If God Will Send His Angels" says: *Then they put Jesus in show business/ Now it's hard to get in the door.*" It seems that rather than digging for Jesus beneath the trash, the Church has unforgivably allowed the trash to come inside and water down whatever there was left of God. Christianity had become commercialized on many levels, and Bono may have been turning over the tables of various modern Christian temple courts, but the most obvious victims of his wrath would be his age-old friends the televangelists.

Whether listening to the *Pop* album, enjoying the Popmart experience or just watching the video, filmed in Mexico City, there is an overwhelming feeling that the book of Ecclesiastes is being made into song to live among us. Irish journalist Stuart Baillie evokes that in his review of the album when he describes it as "watching the world dancing and shagging and shopping and suggesting that it is ultimately joyless." [3]

The first chapter of Ecclesiastes implies that there is nothing to live for under the sun unless you get some kind of connection to what is above the sun (Eccles. 1:9-12:14). The writer says everything goes around and around forever on the same old circle. It's almost like it was written in Ireland. The rain falls into streams and flows into rivers and into the sea and then rises as clouds and blows across the mountains where it falls into streams and then into rivers and into the sea where it rises into clouds and blows across the mountains where it falls...Life can be very much like that. Every day can be the same old drudgery.

WALK ON

12

The wisdom of the teacher, as the writer of Ecclesiastes described, deals with fame as well (Eccles. 1:11). The first chapter also suggests that no one is remembered. It is all vanity. It's pointless even to try to make an impression. And so the teacher wanders around the houses of wealth and pleasure and even philanthropy, but ends up concluding that's all meaningless—unless there is a God (Eccles. 1:2). A vertical connection with the Divine changes everything about how we relate to the horizontal.

Pop and Popmart were like the dramatic soundtrack of that teacher's wanderings. The Old Testament philosopher would have no idea how decadent and ridiculous the trash would have gotten twenty-five hundred years later, but he could have related well to U2's interaction with it. He could have found only empathy with the band's interrogation of the meaninglessness of the horizontal and its constant probing for something else—the search for hope that might be found above the sun to make sense of all the nonsense below it. As U2 "slides down the surface of things," Bono testifies, "I went looking...so much to see." He then confesses, "My heart is where it's always been; my head is somewhere in between." Finally, walking and staggering down the ramps center stage, Bono reached to the heavens, screaming desperately, "Don't walk away!" The teacher could have emerged authentically with this modern day pilgrim and realized the enormous difficulties he has in his longing to get beyond that trash.

Pop could find a home too in the New Testament. It could be a huge theatrical performance of Paul's mission in Athens (Acts 17:16-34). In the early days of the Christian Church, Paul was the great missionary to the gentiles. In the book of Acts, a historical book written by the same doctor, Luke, who wrote a Gospel, we read about the spread of the Christian faith throughout the world of that day. In Chapter 19, Paul has arrived in Athens and is trying to communicate the Gospel into a Greek culture. Before that, he had been preaching in the Jewish synagogues. In Jewish situations, he had been expounding Old Testament theologies like atonement, blood, lambs and sacrifice. When he arrives in Rome, he seems to be giving it much of the same until he realizes it is culturally ineffective. The listeners had no concept of the concepts Paul was using as his hooks.

Paul's response was as wise as a serpent. Jesus told his disciples to be wise as serpents and gentle as doves (Matt. 10:16). Sometimes the Church can be accused of getting these traits the other way around. Not Paul. He readjusted his thinking and rewrote the script to make the truth relevant in another culture. The Church has been slow to do the same. There is an attitude birthed in the enlightenment that says truth is a form of words in a particular order, and there is no wisdom or creativity to poetically take the same truth and describe it in ways more digestible to the world outside Church gates. Paul took his time and walked around the city, imbibing its art and listening to its philosophers and poets. When he gave his sermon to the Athenians, it was on the cutting edge of where that culture was, stating as his points of references all he had seen and heard and read. The truth didn't change; it was just clothed in more relevant outfits.

In some ways, this was U2's reasoning throughout the nineties. In his February 2001 *Hot Press* interview, Bono said: "At the start of the nineties, we realized that to touch and reach people during a new decade, we had to come in a different guise. So we did." [4] Touching and reaching people is so crucial to all that U2 is about. It's not just tickling their ears with pleasant pop songs, but wanting to touch them deep down in their souls in the midst of whatever is going on in their world. It's to assess that world, and point out a few of its dilemmas and dangers, and prod its edifice with a stick to see if there are possible lessons or alternatives. As Bono strode across the Popmart stage, he was not trying in any way to be an evangelical preacher that seeks converts, but he was trying to dialogue with his audience about what a soul might look like and how that soul might be nourished or starved in the contemporary landscape of the world's gods and philosophers and poets.

A trawl through the treasure trove of lyrics on the album would give good evidence to the Athenian nature of the piece. Love was a recurring theme throughout *Pop*, but not in any throwaway silly love song-type vein. As on "Please," there is another conclusion: "*So love is hard/ And love is tough/ But love is not what you are thinking of/ So love is big/ Bigger than us/ But love is not what you're thinking of.*" Love needs to be reassessed in the light of the definitions thrown out daily in our condensed packets of thirty-minute soap operas. "Do You Feel Loved" asks the questions, "*Where are you finding it? How are you defining it?*" Reviewers and interviewers have been writing a lot about Bono's healthy 14-year-old marriage, and perhaps the "*stuck together with God's glue*" line in "Staring at the Sun" hints at some of love's solutions.

The album also deals with eternal issues in songs like "Wake Up Dead Man" and "The Playboy Mansion." The latter is clearly walking around the world's ideas of heaven and showing them up as both transitory and out of reach: "*Don't know if I can hold on/ Don't know if I'm that strong/ Don't know if I can wait that long/ 'Til the colors come flashing/ And the lights go.*" It's about people waiting in the hope of moments of luck to take them out of where they are to where they hope they will find salvation. The song is a weary and desperate acknowledgement that if we are depending on fashion, celebrity, commerce and luck, then we are doomed. Then there is a turn and a twist toward Christian belief and the words of John on Patmos, as written in the New Testament book of Revelation: "*Then there will be no more sorrow/ Then there will be no more shame/ Then there will be no more sorrow/ Then there will be no more pain*" (Rev. 21:3, 4). The alternative to the gods and hopes of the heaven in this age is another kind of mansion altogether.

"Please," with its references to Northern Ireland, seems to be a call for belief to be about more than words and religious prac- tices and the cry for authenticity in the following of Jesus. "*Get up off your knees now please*" seems to be the cry of one who longs for the ideas and clichés of faith to become a living reality. In Northern Ireland, as in many parts of Bible belt America, people have heard the truth of the Gospel until they can almost recite it back to the street preachers. They have heard it. But have they seen it? Get out of your self-indulgent prayer meetings and start to be available to God to answer those prayers.

Elsewhere there are name checks to Michael Jackson, Big Macs, the lottery and even flute bands. As Bono said to Jon Pereles of *The New York Times*, "Musicians, painters, whatever, they have no choice but to describe where they live." [5] So it is all described, reflected on and questioned, and the conclusions are matched up against the alternative Kingdom values spoken of by Jesus. He was suggesting not to store up treasure on earth where it will not last, but to invest in heaven where the contradiction of saving your soul is that you've got to give it away. Thus, when Bono imagines a girl faced with the reality of living her "Last Night on Earth," as one song is titled, she concludes, "*Give it away.*"

When the reviews for *Pop* appeared, there was a preoccupation with all things Christian. In *The Boston Globe*, Jim Sullivan said, "U2 remains identifiable as U2, and this work might also be titled 'Conversations With God'!" [6] He continued, "On *Pop*, U2 finds itself asking us to look for meaning, be it love or faith, amid the chaos and media onslaught of the modern age. 'Last Night on Earth,' with its urgent '*You got to give it away*' refrain, is about living each day as if it might be your last." Mark Brown of *The Orange County (California) Register* finds similar themes: "Not as complex as *Achtung Baby* or *Zooropa*, and more accessible than either of those discs, *Pop* completes a trilogy of searching, questioning works where Bono looks for meaning in a modern world by alternately embracing and disdaining its trappings." [7]

WAKE UP
DEAD MAN

"But you see, David was the first blues singer. As well as praising, he was there shouting at God—you know: 'Where are you when we need you?'…'We're surrounded.'…'Your people are starving.'…'Are you deaf?' That type of thing. He'd be wailing, this militant mind, this poet musician with enough faith to believe he had a deal with God…believed it enough to get angry when it looked like He wasn't coming through." [1]

If ever Bono described himself, it is in those lines from his foreword to John Waters' deep book *Race of Angels*, about U2 and its Irishness. Bono's belief is one that reflects his personality. He's a big character. He is passionate about the things that matter to him, which seem to be his music, his family, his friends and his faith. He is a volatile ball of energy. He is a creative whirlwind of an imagination. He is a dreamer in the apostolic succession of John Lennon, whose honesty he also embraces. But unlike Lennon, he has even more belief in his dreams coming true because he has all his wishes tied up in a dialogue with a transcendent God. So when it all seems to be a nightmare instead of a dream, he is not the kind of man to hide that. He just tells his world and his God what he thinks.

Bono has said that he had been into the Psalms since he was twelve years old. When many children were being turned off from church, he seemed to be able to find interest amid what was becoming increasingly archaic and irrelevant, seeing cinema in the stained glass and heroes in Old Testament stories. King David seems to have been the hero who caught his imagination most. David was one of Israel's most successful kings, a man of deep-seated godliness on a throne that most of the time compromised both religiously and politically. He was also credited with being the writer of a great number of the Psalms. David had a major failure in his life (2 Sam. 11:1-17): He committed adultery with a woman named Bathsheeba and then orchestrated her husband's death in battle. His repentance and reconciliation with God turned out to be another honorable part of David's story. It earthed his holy image. It inspired many Psalms of honesty and humility (Ps. 51).

Bono would call David "a star, the Elvis of the Bible." [2] Bono called himself a fan and could sense empathy between the Israelite's big life and his own rock star absurdities. He also could sense what made the difference in David's successes and failures. He said, "And unusually for such a 'rock star,' with his lust for power, lust for women, lust for life, he had the humility of one who knew his gift worked harder than he ever would." [3] In the end, across twenty-five hundred years of history, the two got to write a song together. When another track was needed for

War, and the band was looking for something more spiritual to complement the political nature of the rest of the album, something that would be a bridge between the album and its predecessor *October*, they found a Psalm and gave it their own musical treatment. "40" was from the Psalm of that number, adding a line from Psalm 5. It became the closing anthem for U2 concerts throughout the eighties, thousands of people leaving stadiums across the world singing an old scriptural hymn.

His public interest in the Psalms, which again was made evident in his references to David as "the first blues singer," [4] made Bono an obvious choice for the publishing house Canongate to introduce the book of Psalms in an intriguing series of books called the *Pocket Canons*. The idea for publishing the books of the Bible individually came when someone went looking for the Song of Songs for his wife's birthday gift and was told that it was only possible to buy all sixty-six books of the Bible. Then to add another dimension to the ancient literature, modern writers and poets, novelists and songwriters were asked to write their thoughts, almost like little reviews, as introductions to the books. Writers such as Faye Weldon, Blake Morrison, Peter Ackroyd, Ruth Rendell and P.D. James, as well as the likes of singers Nick Cave and Bono, got to dialogue at some level with St. Mark, St. John, St. Paul, Isaiah and, of course, King David.

The publicity for the project was enormous. The Bible was on display all around bookstores. Most of the broadsheet newspapers did reviews and articles. Evangelical Christians had been campaigning for years in a wide array of projects to get the Bible back into people's hands. The Bible was back in the news and in conversation. Prayers had been answered. Then, in a twist, the company that produced the books was not hailed as an answer to prayer but was taken to court for blasphemy. The fundamentalist end of the Church was unhappy that the introductions were not always glowing in their support of Scripture. Some writers would question the literal belief in certain events and would not claim to have had any Christian conversion from reading their designated book. Some admitted to reading it for the first time. Yet most of the writers were enthusiastic, not only about the books as literature but as good, life-changing advice.

What the opposition to the *Pocket Canons* exposed was a lack of faith among those who claimed faith. If, as many of these fundamentalists believed, God's Word was unique and special, holding with it some kind of authority beyond any other literary work, then there seems to have been nothing to fear in having it thrown into discussion, discourse and even disagreement. It is a surprising outworking of a belief in an all-powerful God to be so defensive and protective of Him and His Word.

Bono's contribution appeared in the second batch of books released. It was his introduction that drew the most publicity. The UK's *Sunday Express* printed the whole introduction. Again, Bono is seeing much of himself and his belief and his art in David. He also writes about the Psalms that he has a particular empathy with: "Abandonment, displacement is the stuff of my favorite Psalms. The Psalter may be a font of gospel music, but for me, it's in his despair that the Psalmist really reveals the nature of his special relationship with God. Honesty, even to the point of anger. 'How long, Lord? Wilt thou hide thyself forever?' (Ps. 89) or 'Answer me when I call' (Ps. 5)." [5] Bono likened the Psalmist to bluesman Robert Johnston and said the Psalms prepared him for the honesty he later discovered in Leonard Cohen and John Lennon. The blues, and indeed full frontal naked honesty, has not been predominant in the worship of the modern evangelical Church. Where the Church has seemed to be growing in the western world, it has been nurtured by the sensational. At

> Bono takes it all on. He longs for heaven on earth and tells his God he is tired of waiting.

the same time that U2 was exposing the absurdity of fame and the deception that big is always better, many churches were being sucked into its absurdity and were seduced by the success of numbers and the spectacular event. Healing extravaganzas and sell-out worship concerts where the worship leader became a new kind of pop star was the modern day order. Triumphant victory was the best sales pitch, and the songs of the faithful became obsessed with God, high and lifted up, conquering all and dealing with every ailment physical, emotional and spiritual at the touch of a hand.

U2 was like an antidote to that reality. The band members looked the dark side of life right in the eye. They never felt a need for glib solutions or shortcuts to what the Kingdom was taking time to bring. Believers in the Christian faith who, as a result, are deeply engaged in the writings of the Old and New Testament are caught in the horns of dilemma many times. Believing these ancient manuscripts of Scripture to be the inspired Word of God (2 Tim. 3:16, 17), they often are thrown by the reality of the news on television clashing with Divine revelation. An example is every Christmas, when those angels glide above the astonished shepherds and tell them, "Glory to God in the highest/ And on earth peace to men/ On whom his favour rests" (Luke 2:14).This peace on earth usually clashes, literally, violently with the year-end reviews of twelve months of tragedy, disaster, violent crime, terrorist atrocities and war. Where is the peace? What were those angels talking about?

How do you answer such questions and not play gymnastics with Scripture or ignore the reality of the news? It's a hard position for a Christian whose worldview has been dictated by the seamlessness of modernity. U2's post-modern worldview, though no better or worse than modernity, allows mystery and confusion to sit alongside faith. As Bono put it to Neil McCormick: "Belief and confusion are not mutually exclusive; I believe that belief gives you a direction in the confusion. But you don't see the full picture. That's the point. That's what faith is. You can't see it. It comes back to instinct. Faith is just up the street. Faith and instinct, you can't just rely on them. You have to beat them up. You have to pummel them to make sure they can withstand it, to make sure they can be trusted." [6]

Instead of separating the tussle of his faith and the confusion, Bono is always able to bring the two eyeball to eyeball. That's what happens in "Wake Up Dead Man" and "Peace on Earth." If you are watching the 1998 year in review, in the midst of your children's nativity plays, how do you reconcile the twenty-seven lives so violently and needlessly ended by a bomb on a Saturday afternoon in a market town with the song of the angels? Honesty, vulnerability and a good amount of courageous faith allow you to cry out in your bewilderment and not lose your belief in the process. These things allow you to wrestle your faith rather than lose it. They allow you to cry out, "*Jesus, could you take the time/ To throw a drowning man a line/ Peace on earth.*" Bono takes it all on. He longs for heaven on earth and tells his God he is tired of waiting. He asks His God to answer the cries of those who have lost their children. He concludes by telling Jesus that the words of that Christmas nativity stick in his throat, and he asks Him what it is worth—"this peace on earth."

This is why the Church needs Bono. This is why everybody needs Bono. He is willing to take what he believes and the world around him, and wrestle with them and not let them go. "Peace on Earth" is upfront and without apologies. It's a rant at God. It sits precariously close to slushy and sentimental when he names some of the victims of the Omagh bombing and links them with Christmas peace words. It works because the sentimentality is given the roughest of edges by the confrontation with God. It is by no means a new theme on a U2 record. It could be seen as a direct follow-up to the last track on *Pop*, "Wake Up Dead Man," when Jesus again is asked to help him because he feels alone in the world, "and a f***ed-up world it is, too."

For most Christians, the use of the "F" word would not help the medicine go down. Initially, the song seems to portray Jesus as dead and impotent with His hands tied behind his back, unable to bring any help to a troubled world. Closer inspection sheds a little more light. Struggling with why things are as they are and why God does nothing about it is common to everyone at one time or another. "Wake Up Dead Man" is trying to make sense, without actually making any, of the problems of pain and suffering under the eye of a loving God. It is the prayerful seeking of

> U2's post-modern worldview allows mystery and confusion to sit alongside faith.
>
> WAKE UP DEAD MAN

help and wanting a reminder of how things will be in eternity. It confesses belief in God as Creator—"*He made the world in seven*"—and in Jesus as the "Boss." It's a ranting plea to intervene and bring a solution to humanity's conundrum of evil: "*Are you working on something new?*"

Bono said of the song: "It's the end of the century, and it's a century where God is supposed to be dead. Seeing the world in two dimensions doesn't have the appeal that it had for a lot of people. People want to believe, but they're angry, and I picked up on that anger. If God is not dead, there are some questions we want to ask him. I'm a believer, but that doesn't mean I don't get angry about these things."

This dynamic of dilemma has been at work in U2's songwriting for many years. *Boy* was an honest struggle with adolescence, and even the charismatic enthusiasm of *October* had its admission of failure. "Sunday Bloody Sunday" took the voice of the Psalmist in the despairing cry, *"How long must we sing this song?"* "I Still Haven't Found What I'm Looking For" would become quintessentially U2's soul view. Another song from *The Joshua Tree*, "Bullet the Blue Sky," would be cut from an Old Testament lamenting rock. After a trip to Central America, where he witnessed the horrific things the country was doing to the native population, Bono returned to Dublin and asked The Edge to do his best to put the rage of El Salvador through his amplifiers. There perhaps has never been a more turbulent and war-like rock track in the history of music. In the midst of Bono's lyrics, there is an almost throw-away line that might just be the crucial clue to "Wake Up Dead Man," "Peace on Earth" and so much more. Bono sings, *"Jacob wrestled with the angel, and the angel was overcome."*

In another Old Testament story, Jacob was a scoundrel, a man who deceived everyone he came in contact with, from his father to his brother to his father-in-law. Somehow the grace of God "sees beauty in ugly things" and "sees goodness in everything." We are told that Jacob and a man tumbled and wrestled one entire night. In the dawn, Jacob realized something supernatural was happening and would not let his assailant go until he blessed him. The mysterious aggressor eventually was understood to be God, and Jacob got a new name, Israel, which means "wrestled with God." A nation was born (Gen. 32:22-32).

It is that same wrestling that Bono has been doing in his art. He has never let go. Since the early days in the fervent and zealous and a lot more naive Christian fellowship in Dublin, Bono has tried to make sense of his unflinching faith in God and Christian redemption and hope. He never hid it from the difficult issues that faith has to wrestle with in the unbelievable world he has seen as a rock star, humanitarian and courter of popes and presidents and prime ministers.

LEAP OF FAITH

In 1988, as U2 promoted *The Joshua Tree* and was building up
the idea of embarking on its study of America's heartland, the
band members found themselves on the roof of a Los Angeles
hotel for a photo shoot with Anton Corbjin. It was a place that
dropped a seed into the fertile imagination of Bono, a seed that
would take some twelve years to be harvested. At one end of the
roof, there was another building just a few meters away. It
seemed so close that apparently The Edge told Bono he could
reach it. "If you have the faith and really believe you can do it,
then you'll make it," he said. [1] Thirteen years later, Bono took
journalist Sean O'Hagan to the edge of that same roof and
echoed The Edge's thought: "It would take a good run up." [2] The
building on which they stood was the Million Dollar Hotel.

The hotel fascinated Bono. More than just the roof, it was the
clientele that hung around the lobby and lived in the hotel that
captured Bono's attention the most. Built long ago as the biggest

and best hotel in America and given its title to attract rich travelers, the Million Dollar Hotel had become the hangout of the underbelly of LA life. Those on welfare and Social Security would congregate there, and Bono's mind raced about those people, their stories, their lives. This was a movie.

For twelve years following that initial seed, Bono developed the story. He brought on board Nicholas Klein, who would eventually write the script, and Wim Wenders, who would be the director and producer. Wenders is most famous for his movie *Wings of Desire*, and his movies *Until the End of the World* and *Far Away So Close* have obvious links with U2 as they share song titles. The band also contributed a duet with Sinead O'Connor, "I Am Not Your Baby," to yet another Wenders movie, *The End of Violence*. It was this movie that Klein probably was best known for writing, and the three came together to work on and improve Bono's original idea for the film *Million Dollar Hotel*.

Million Dollar Hotel was a slow burn. Mel Gibson, its star, could not find himself anywhere further from *Braveheart*, *The Patriot* or *Lethal Weapon*. The film is about freaky characters with darkness and a lot of soul. Bono does with his storyline what he so often does with his lyrics. Like a magpie, he goes about knitting together scraps of ideas into one whole piece. In *Million Dollar Hotel*, there are a few Bono obsessions. Hotel culture is the most obvious. Bono pointed out repeatedly during interviews how he knew hotels rather well from all the band's world tours and how he'd even bought one, The Clarence, in Dublin.

His fascination with John Lennon is exposed in the brilliant performance of Peter Stormare as Dixie. The character basically lives out Bono's John Lennon fantasy, believing to have written the Beatles songs and at one point declaring that it was the first time he'd left the hotel since December 1980. Television is also a recurring theme in throwaway scenarios, where it seems to be omnipresent; in the way the TV media descend on the hotel to deal with the art scam; and in the confession of the killer, which appears not in a police report but in an interview replayed on prime time news.

The trumpet player on the film's soundtrack, Jon Hassell, described the film as being a "screwball tragedy," [3] but there are moments of real beauty, oft tenderness and glimpses of fulfil-ment and how life could be if love had its way. Here is another one of Bono's constant themes, maybe one that is appearing more and more as the years go by—unconditional love. He him-self said: "It was initially going to be a play about a leap of faith, but then it mutated into something bigger and darker. I'd call it a dark fable on the redemptive power of love." [4]

This is where the light shines in *Million Dollar Hotel*. Tom Tom, the narrator, is the most lovable and innocent angel-like idiot and falls in love with the vulnerable and beautiful prostitute Eloise. Played stunningly by Jeremy Davies and Milla Jovovich, it is in the interaction of these two characters that the film finds its soul. In each other, they find a love that neither of them has ever known. Tom Tom is so innocent he really is not even sure what sex is and is certainly not pursuing Eloise for any momentary wantonness. Eloise has never known anyone who just wants her for herself. They both find the redemption that Bono speaks of in one another. Bono is speaking about how earthly love—which he often has referred to as a miracle in itself—can make broken

WALK ON

14

people whole. But there is the transcendent idea of Divine love shadowing the whole escapade.

> "It was initially going to be a play about a leap of faith, but then it mutated into something bigger and darker. I'd call it a dark fable on the redemptive power of love."

Bono's storytelling always repels any hints of a happy ending. The movie begins with its most successful cinematic scene, where the camera pans across downtown LA and fixes upon the twenty-foot letters that spell the movie's title. As this happens, U2's "The First Time," originally on *Zooropa*, sets the storyline and mood. The use of songs is another one of the movie's most successful tools. In "The First Time," the prodigal gets the keys to the Kingdom, and just as Bono says he could not sing such a happy ending but wanted to look at the other angle, so it is in the movie. Tom Tom, with his salvation assured in the arms of Eloise, runs across that roof with the most peaceful and joyous smile as he waves to Eloise—who is at the roof door trying to save him. He takes the leap, a leap out of this world, or a leap into the next world. As he falls, he says, "Wow, after I jumped it occurred to me: Life is perfect. Life is the best. Full of magic and beauty, opportunity and television and surprises, lots of surprises, yeah. And then there's the best stuff, of course better than anyone ever made up because it's real…"

Million Dollar Hotel is yet another study in the tangled web of darkness and light that life is all about. It is a web that shimmers and shines much more in the mind of a Christian who has to deal with all the contradictions of the juxtaposition of those shadows and shades. There are similarities to a much more successful Hollywood flick of the time, *Magnolia*, which looks at the darker shades of the underside and then breaks through with the brightest moments of illumination. The need for salvation and redemption is deeply embedded in both movies.

Art is everything that the members of U2 have been about, exploring the world and faith and love in whatever creative ways stimulate them and leaving the door ajar for whatever insight they stumble upon. Bono's idea of a film script was a natural outworking of that. It was no surprise that the final product was independent, mysterious, poetic, divine, provocative and lingering. If the film did anything, it left deep-seeded emotions and a haunting sense of love for the characters for weeks after it left the cinema. It was the speed of the chase that foxed the audience, especially those who had been attracted by Mel Gibson's FBI role.

The soundtrack to *Million Dollar Hotel* came before the movie. The soundtrack gained credibility even before it was fully understood by its use in the film. While only three of the songs got a U2 credit, three others include Bono with either The Million Dollar Hotel Band or, as on "Falling at Your Feet," with Daniel Lanois. "Falling at Your Feet" is strong and insightful in the vein of Bob Dylan's "Gonna Serve Somebody." Bono layers image upon image of people "falling at your feet." The lyrics include some of Bono's most clever one-liners: "*Every teenager with acne/*

WALK ON

14

Every face that's spoiled by beauty/ Every adult tamed by duty…/ Every life that has no end/ Every knee not ready to bend…" Whose feet they are falling at and why comes through in the song's conclusion: *"Teach me to surrender/ Not my will, Thy will."*

It is a wonderful piece of Christian hymnody. Bono, as he had done before, seems to be delving into Paul's letter to the church in Philippi. If "Still Haven't Found…" could be linked with Philippians 3, then "Falling at Your Feet" is very much rooted in Philippians 2:9-11. In this passage, Paul is encouraging those at the church at Philippi to humble themselves as servants as Christ did. It is about Christ's surrendering to the will of God, and having done so, Paul concludes that "God exalted Him to the highest place and gave Him the name that is above every name, that at the name of Jesus every knee should bow, in heaven and earth and under the earth, and every tongue confess that Jesus is Lord, to the glory of God the Father."

This song, in its gentle, understated way, takes us to the grand culmination of history. Here, falling at the feet of God, is every lonely, broken, confused, tragic loser or seeming winner who doesn't even realize it. In such a moment, the conclusion comes, *"How can we stand? Whom shall we trust?"* The solution is in surrender: *"Not my will, Thy will"* (Matt. 26:39). The movie does not use much of the song or its conclusion. It is in this song, and not in the final cut of Bono's storyline, where that "leap of faith" is found. It is a song about surrender. It's a song about letting go to transcendence and finding some grace. From the pop star to the prisoner, everything one day will fall at the feet of God. Ultimately how do you find salvation? Surrender.

Like so much of U2's work, this theme can be traced back through the band's entire catalog. Surrender has been a constant theme in songs such as "I Will Follow" and "Out of Control" on *Boy*, "Surrender" on *War* and "The Last Night on Earth" on *Pop*. Ever-present in U2 members' lives and songs has been this secret of spiritual living, bowing down to a higher power and the losing self to gain eternity. In a *Rolling Stone* interview at the end of 2000, Bono said: "Christ says, 'If you love your life too much, you've already lost it' (Luke 9:24). Which is an interesting one. As a younger man, I remember I didn't understand what that meant because I loved life. You're holding on so tight to it you're incapable of doing anything with it. It's about fear." [5] There are signs here of Bono's maturing as a human being as well as his ongoing meditation on Scripture.

Whatever we make of the more-than-reasonable soundtrack or the intrigue of the characters and jazzy storyline, Bono's first foray into movies did not see as much commercial success as had his band. *Million Dollar Hotel* was released in Europe in 2000. By the time it reached the United States in the first months of 2001, the reviews had been written, the critics had dismissed it with all other rock star attempts at Hollywood, and even the star of the show, Mel Gibson, was denouncing it as boring. It only hit a few big screens in the United States. Apart from its Silver Bear Award at the Berlin Film Festival, it's safe to say that it is Bono's biggest failure since *Rattle and Hum*, that other movie. Like with *Rattle and Hum*, though, there is no reason to dismiss *Million Dollar Hotel*, especially if you are a U2 fan. The movie is a slow-paced mixture of love story, art scam and whodunit all wrapped up in more than its fair share of the bizarre and offbeat. But there are characters, beauty, sadness and an ecstatic sense of salvation in here that linger with the harder-working viewer for a long time after the credits have rolled.

GRACE

When U2 released its first album of the new millennium, *All That You Can't Leave Behind*, it was almost as big a culture shock for the U2 traveler as *Achtung Baby* had been a decade earlier. Somewhere between the last concert of the Popmart tour in March 1998 in Johannesburg and the middle of 2000, the technology took leave and U2 stood, once more, as naked as the proverbial jaybird—bass, drums, three chords and the truth. In the *Achtung Baby* video, Bono mischievously looked at the camera and said, "I learned how to lie." Here the members of U2 were learning how to tell the truth again, revealing themselves again, dreaming it up all over again—again! They were going back to find the future. *All That You Can't Leave Behind* was no repeat of past glories; it was a rediscovery of U2 in the primary colors of their sound and their spirit of honesty and vulnerability.

After an album called *Pop*, they finally had found pop. Now all the harshness of the preceding trilogy was gone, and what remained was the purity of the song without clutter—just the most gorgeous melodies, dashes of great playing and Bono's voice giving its best performance ever. Every track was a potential hit single, fully exposed in all its beauty. Beauty was one adjective rarely used in a U2 review in the nineties. But beautiful this was. One review even described Larry's drumming as "gorgeous." Along with the technology, the shades and horns had also been thrown out with the trash. Writer David Dark has said that on the first listen to U2 albums, people are always concerned that they have lost their faith, and then as they listen and allow the songs to play around in their minds and heart and soul, they wish they were as Christian as U2. *All That You Can't Leave Behind* did not need any time to resonate with the soul. This was as upfront about faith as the band had been in twenty years.

It was quite a reinvention. What were the reasons? There may have been many. The cynic may have touched on something if he said one of them was commercial. Though *Pop* and Popmart probably would have been hailed as a success had they happened to any other band, U2 experienced a disappointment commercially at the end of the nineties. The band may have had a need to regain the bigger audience. The guys of U2 would never settle for being The Rolling Stones, touring greatest hits packages long after their artistic zenith. It was important that they remained relevant, accepted for their new work as much as their past. A more immediate sound may have been an important consideration as a new album project got under way. The marketing of the album and the Elevation tour that would follow were strategically different. A few smaller gigs, supposedly for the fans to see them in an intimate setting, had a publicity strategy and helped the band rekindle the fires of starting again.

WALK ON

15

The return to an arena tour in the United States as opposed to playing in stadiums as in recent years was to guarantee a big demand for tickets, a demand that would grow, not diminish. The album and tour showed a band spilling over the brim with the inspiration, fresh enthusiasm, and best songs and performances of a band that was hailed as the best on the planet more than twenty years after it began.

There is a story, truth or myth, that during the Popmart tour, U2 found a dingy little room in which to rehearse, and without much gear available, the band members made do with what amps they had and practiced the best they could. In the middle of this makeshift rehearsal, their cool, cutting-edge, dance groove sampler Howie B happened in upon them. After listening for a few moments, he asked them, in not too Presbyterian language, what on earth was that amazing noise they were creating. The techno boy had been blown away by the stark naked drums, bass and guitar of a rock 'n' roll band. Apparently, from that gig on, during the tour Howie B drew back the number of technological loops and sounds he was adding to the brew. Perhaps this was a turning point.

Author Salman Rushdie recalls a lunch at Bono's home in Killiney, south Dublin, when Wim Wenders "announced that artists must no longer use irony. Plain speaking, he argued, was necessary now. Communication should be direct, and anything that might create confusion should be eschewed." [1] U2 responded by taking the irony even further on *Pop*, but then they realized Wenders had a point and they should follow their cinematic friend's advice into the next phase.

Though not recording, this was a seriously busy "down time" for U2. As well as the soundtrack and movie *Million Dollar Hotel*, they took part in The Belfast Agreement Campaign, helped launch an Amnesty International petition in support of the Universal Declaration on Human Rights, inducted Bruce Springsteen into the Rock 'n' Roll Hall of Fame, had three babies and released *The Best of 1980-1990* compilation, whose "Sweetest Thing" single was a huge hit. Bono sang on Kirk Franklin's "Lean on Me" and Wyclef Jean's "New Day," which benefited NetAid charity. Bono also had a dinner in his home for Northern Irish politician John Hume in commemoration of the Nobel Peace Prize he and David Trimble won, met former President Bill Clinton when he came to Dublin, and had an audience with the pope where he traded his glasses for a set of rosary beads.

The meeting with the pope was part of the Jubilee 2000 campaign that delayed U2's next album. The spirit of Jubilee 2000 could have contributed to the depth and openness of the soul in the band's next recordings and performances. Even as the members masqueraded in their hedonistic persona of the nineties, they continued to publicize Amnesty and support many other causes such as War Child, which had the focus of its attention on Sarajevo. That war-torn city's name was the title of arguably the best song on the *Passengers* album, in which all four band members were involved, along with their producer, Brian Eno, as a more involved collaborator. They even played a gig there in 1997. Even though Bono's voice was in tatters, the gig was broadcast on BBC Radio One.

As the end of the millennium neared, many organizations were exploiting the landmark event and possibility of the biggest party in history. From champagne companies to local government, money was being spent or earned in all kinds of reckless ways. That justice organizations would attempt to use the date to achieve worthwhile results would help redeem a New Year's Eve that would end up as singer/songwriter Aimee Mann once described the Fourth of July: "a waste of gunpowder and sky." [2] Bono wanted to exploit the calendar for the good of humanity, not just the pleasure drives of a hedonistic west. The guys of U2 are rock stars and live in a rock star stratosphere. They enjoy that world. Perhaps they even indulge in that world in a way that might be judged as a little excessive. Yet they never lose sight of what's important. They never strive for it or put it in the wrong end of the ladder of their priorities. Sure, on millennium night, these four Dublin guys partied with the best of them, but their individual enjoyment was never more important than the world issues that have been so much a part of their legend.

Jubilee 2000 was an interfaith effort that began in the offices of Christian Aid and soon became an all-encompassing campaign. At last, a Christian organization pioneered the cause and, as happens too rarely, showed that if something is essentially Christian, even those who might not hold to a Christian worldview or belief can benefit from the teachings of Jesus, which should be for the betterment of everyone. The idea of Jubilee is found in Leviticus 25, in the Old Testament, where God commands that every fifty years there should be a special year for liberty and restoration. People who had slid down the economic scales for whatever reason got a fresh start, a theme that is central to the whole message of the Bible—grace. Bono would later say that you can't write lyrics about debt relief, but then point to the song "Grace," which closes *All That You Can't Leave Behind*: "It's about the right to begin again, the right to be free of your past. That's grace. So, yes, you can write lyrics about debt relief." In this phrase, Bono overlays the crux of Christ's Gospel to the soul, which is souls being saved by the grace of God alone and having an opportunity for a new birth, with the crux of Christ's Gospel to the body and justice in the bringing about of a heaven on earth.

Leviticus 25:35 says: "If one of your countrymen becomes poor and is unable to support himself among you, help him as you would an alien or temporary resident, so that he can continue to live among you. Do not take interest of any kind from him, but fear God so that your countrymen may continue to live among you. You must not lend money at interest or sell food for profit." You will not find these verses in the Hit Parade of sermon texts being preached in evangelical churches on a Sunday morning. But with the modern global village, the Jubilee 2000 campaign took this neglected principle and applied it to countries trapped in a never-ending cycle of debt repayments. The money given to Third World charities every year falls way short of the interest repayments those countries send back to the west.

Bono was drawn in by his interest in Scripture and his applying Scripture to justice and peace. The links that must have convinced him to participate in Jubilee 2000 were his involvement in Band Aid and Live Aid, and the month he and Ali spent in Ethiopia working in a relief camp. They had given him a heart and a rage for the cause. The fact that the $200 million raised by 1985's greatest show on earth was about the same amount African nations owed in debt repayments every five days must have brought back some of the rage and shown an older and wiser Bono that more than a bandage was needed. The cause of the gash needed healing. Providing relief was a good thing, but dealing with the very structures of poverty was a much greater cause.

It had been ten years since Bono had put himself on the front line of the abuse and suspicion rock stars receive when they put their names to causes. Sting got negative publicity for his

For a long time, Bono and the rest of the U2 guys were amused by the absurdity and obscenity of how important rock stardom had become.

GRACE

involvement in the Amazon Rain Forest cause and, of course, the members of U2 stepped back from being protest rock singers at the end of the eighties because of the disparaging reaction their sincerity had caused. Ten years later, Bono seemed to be less concerned with the snide press he might receive than he was with the potential result he might be able to achieve.

For a long time, Bono and the rest of the U2 guys were amused by the absurdity and obscenity of how important rock stardom had become. He had laughed about this and at himself before the public on the Zoo TV tour. Now he was seeing how foolish it seemed that this Dublin singer should have the clout to affect

WALK ON

15

world powers. He said, when Jubilee 2000 earned him an audience with the Pope: "U2's music has taken me on some odd diversions, but this has got to be the maddest and most absurd experience of my life." [3] Laughable it might be, but Bono was cunning enough to exploit the seemingly foolish position his music had given him. Jamie Drummond of Christian Aid, who recruited Bono for the "foot in the door" job, seems to have been strategic in his planning. Drummond and Jubilee 2000 recognized that in the era of celebrity, they needed someone to catch the imagination of the media. He said: "Bono got meetings with people that we couldn't meet with. If you're looking for the X factor, it is that we managed to win over the attention of the media, which usually ignore a cause like this. And that was through Bono." [4]

This is the kind of potent contribution that Bono, as a Christian, can make to the world through being a rock star with belief and convictions. Had U2 given up at the command of its well-intentioned spiritual gurus in the early eighties, who would Jamie Drummond have been able to turn to? It was Bono's Christian faith that was the bridge to Christian Aid. It was his radical political and justice beliefs rooted in the following of Christ via the likes of Martin Luther King, Jr., that caused him to be up for it. He is a classic example of a Christian living his life in the real world and having a natural influence in that world. Bono hasn't done Gospel altar calls during "40" at the encore of concerts, but he has been out there in the flowing tide of the real world, sometimes bouncing about in its stormier seas. In the end, he got the opportunity to be the spokesman of a campaign that would affect a significant portion of God's planet, finding some justice and hope and literally saving people's lives. Many would accuse Bono of doing nothing for Christ and being ashamed of the Gospel. In Jubilee 2000, Bono lived it out in the heat of the world's spotlight.

It was that very flowing tide where Jesus had commanded his disciples to live. Out there where the city gambles. Where no one believes. Out there among the thieves. In the face of abuse and mockery. Where love violently dies. Out there at their daily Calvary, to take up their crosses and follow. Not to holler but to follow. If only Jesus had said to Peter, "Pray this prayer and withdraw from the world and make sure you preach in every song." He didn't. He said, "Follow me into a daily dynamic of dilemma where they will misunderstand you and castigate you and call you all kinds of things. It'll be messy, and every decision will not always be on the white or black side of grey, but follow me. Get involved. Where I walked."

Bono's place in the world gave him a big enough foot to be able to stick in some big and few important doors. The organizers of Jubilee 2000 were stunned at his commitment. Bono was not going to do a rock star conscience saver and do a concert, raise a lot of money and give a week's news profile. Maybe he saw he could be Martin Luther King for a while. He wanted the bigger job. Drummond says: "We expected that [Bono's involvement] might be concerts and records, but it turned out Bono's a very brilliant political lobbyist." [5] He was going to get his hands dirty, at least as dirty as presidents, popes and prime ministers get. It was expensive white collar dirty, but it was the equivalent of the blood, sweat and tears of the corridors of political power. Bono walked through the doors of the houses of political might and took on the world's finest economists and bank managers. Holly

Peterson put it well in the January 2000 *Newsweek*, which featured Bono on its cover. She explained that she called financier David Rockefeller and UN Ambassador Richard Holbrooke. She says: "I said I had a kooky proposal. 'I'm going to bring a rock star into your office in weird sunglasses to talk about Third World debt.' They were sceptical. But within five minutes, they were floored by his breadth of knowledge." [6]

Christians have been bringing about social change and campaigning for justice for centuries. Martin Luther King, Jr., of course, is one great example. In the United Kingdom, William Wilberforce campaigned for the abolition of slavery for twenty years before he achieved success. In the first half of the nineteenth century, Lord Shaftesbury entered politics not long after his conversion to Christianity, and he spent most of his political career dealing with humanitarian issues, especially working conditions. He got a ten-hour work limitation for children, got a ban on woman and children having to work underground, and improved many other employment conditions.

As the millennium ended, Jubilee 2000, with significant help from Bono, had encouraged the seven richest nations to promise the cancellation of $110 billion in debt that possibly would benefit some forty-one countries. There were still many conditions that would allow the rich nations to stall on implementing this, and it was still considered to be an opportunity missed to deal with the horrific effects of such crippling debts. U2 continued to use the concerts in the Elevation tour, which began in March 2001 in Florida, to encourage fans to mail or email President George Bush and other decision-makers, asking them to take more action on the debt that will have caused the deaths of a million children during U2's three-month tour. They were also campaigning for action against the HIV/ AIDS crisis in Africa.

Bono often has said it is his Catholic guilt that drives him. Just as this is another veil to protect him from being labeled in any particular camp—he asked if the pope was aware he wasn't a Catholic before he met him—there is truth in the statement. It is Bono's spiritual provocation that will not allow him to lie back and enjoy his own luxury. His obsession with Jesus Christ prods him to keep stirring up anything he can to improve the world. As he told Olaf Tyaransen in a *Hot Press* interview in November 2000: "I can't live with acquiescence. I can't make peace with myself or the world. I just can't. To me, it's like rolling over. So in doing things like Jubilee 2000, I do feel better for actually feeling that I'm getting my hands around the throat of something I care about." [7]

That idea of grace that Bono mentioned as a theology for Jubilee 2000 has been a constant phrase on the lips of Bono in more recent years. Bono even sent a copy of Philip Yancey's book *What's So Amazing About Grace* to Oasis' Noel Gallagher after the two had an in-depth conversation about faith in 2001. In a *Q* article just before the release of *All That You Can't Leave Behind*, Bono says he was always more into grace than karma. [8] If karma was what it was all about, he was coming back as a frog! Sean O'Hagan, in his detailed article on the events of the Belfast Agreement Yes concert, says Bono was chatting with Unionist politician David Trimble about the merits of the hymn "Amazing Grace." Even before that, when asked by British broadcaster and television celebrity Chris Evans what song he would sing if the world was about to end, Bono immediately responded "Amazing

Grace," and continued, "how sweet the sound." Then there is the final song on *All That You Can't Leave Behind*, "Grace": "*It's the name for a girl/ It's also a thought that changed the world.*" In concert from here on, Bono would name check "Amazing Grace" neatly into the lyrics of "I Will Follow." That makes an interesting dovetailing of the U2 career, as "I Will Follow" was the first

> "It's lukewarm believers that drive me out of the Church."
>
> — GRACE

track on the band's first album, and "Grace" was the final track on U2's most recent album at that point.

The spirit of this grace came through in an interview Bono did with Irish journalist Joe Jackson about a Samuel Beckett Film Festival at the beginning of 2001 in Dublin. Jackson touched on the underlying sense of attitude within the U2 camp, as its decade hidden behind the shades of irony faded and gave birth to yet another reinvention. [9] Throughout the interview, Jackson constantly tried to caress and collide Beckett and Bono with each other. Under the surmise that these two Irish writers are very strange bedfellows, he probed Bono to conclude that they have nothing in common. As with the vast majority of interviews with Bono, the God question was raised, and Jackson pointed out that it's a godless universe that Beckett depicts and this must leave Bono cold. "No, it doesn't because a lot of my friends are atheists," he responded. "It's lukewarm believers that drive me out of the Church. It's the big questions, isn't it? If there's a God, it's serious; if there's not a God, it's even more serious. And Beckett did at least approach the question." [10] Bono's respect for the atheist is refreshing. Many believers distance themselves from those with differing views on God, sometimes even within different churches. Bono makes them his friends and then makes himself accountable to them. He has fellowship and sharpens his faith against those with whom he doesn't agree because they are discussing the same issues.

Jackson quoted Beckett as having believed that "to be an artist is to fail as no other dare fail. Failure is his world." [11] Bono immediately responded: "I really identify with that because what I think Beckett is getting at is that you must get the fear of failure out of the way. Once you become a better failure, you can really go places. For example, I have discussed this in the past. The constrictions of being cool. It's useless. And Lou Reed said that to me. He grew up in the fifties with the fifties idea of what it means to be cool. It's a stranglehold." Jackson then asked if U2 had burst beyond that stranglehold. "We played it cool for ten years." Had the band members finally freed themselves to be hot and bothered? "Yeah, we are! But at the start of the nineties, we realized that to touch and reach people during a new decade, we had to come in a different guise. So we did. Now the real challenge is to turn up without a mask. And I must tell you, it's not as easy to take the shades off as I thought it would be."

Here is the secret to the reinvention. The U2 members had lost the need to succeed and had come to terms with being relaxed in failure if failure should come. Isn't this what cool really is? Not minding if the world thinks you are cool. Just being faithful to you, no matter what the consequences. Not that failure was about to descend upon U2. "Beautiful Day" hit number one on the UK charts. The forty-year-olds reigned supreme.

"Beautiful Day" was an interesting opening track for *All That You Can't Leave Behind*. The last track on U2's nineties catalog, as the entire world seemed caught up in a frenzy of apocalyptic doom and gloom, fearful about the ending of a millennium, was "Wake Up Dead Man." It was as though Jesus was in the tomb after his crucifixion, lifeless, with the disciples letting go of all hope. John Lennon's words "the dream is over" come to mind. "Beautiful Day" is like an ecstatic proclamation that Peter and James might have sung just after Mary had come back to the disciples' hiding place with resurrection news. The biblical image used may be the dove going out from the ark to bring back the leaf that informed Noah that the old world had ended and a new one could begin. But even that depicts the whole celebratory mood of dead man waking up and a whole new Kingdom being birthed. The album and the Elevation tour would see a new resurrection shuffle of a mood in the U2 camp.

As well as the biblical reference in "Beautiful Day" and the band's theological take on "Grace," the whole album is drenched in an upfront spirituality. The cover even has a clue as to the state of U2's spiritual temperature as it features a cryptic Bible verse from Jeremiah 33:3. The band had gotten Steve Averill to doctor the cover shot of the band members taken at Charles De Gaule Airport and change the gate number behind them to read

J33-3. Bono called the verse God's telephone number as it reads, "Call to me and I will answer you and tell you great and unsearchable things you do not know."

That cover shot of the band members in a place of departure with their baggage beside them and Bono checking his passport depicts traveling. Symbolically, the music was leaving in other directions, and the technology was staying behind. There has to be more, though, and "Walk On" gives an obvious clue with a clever twist and a familiar phrase, "*You're packing your suitcase for a place none of us has been/ A place that has to be believed to be seen.*" The song, dedicated to Burmese human rights campaigner Aung San Suu Kyi, does seem to live in two dimensions. Bono is always running and climbing and crawling toward what he is looking for here on earth. A world of freedom and justice has to be first believed before it can be achieved.

It is another song about these guys hanging on to the fraying thread of faith in spite of what is going on around them: "*And if the darkness is to keep us apart/ And if the daylight feels a long way off/ And if your glass heart should crack/ And for a second you turn back/ Oh, no, be strong.*" Bono's perseverance that he yearns to transmit to Suu Kyi may have its basis in his love of Scripture. When the apostle Paul says nothing on this earth can separate us from the love of God (Rom. 8:38, 39), it is a promise they could see through the many dark nights of the soul.

But the cover and title have yet another, spiritual and heavenly dimension. When U2 sang "Walk On" at the telethon for the heroes of the tragic events in New York, Washington and Pennsylvania on September 11, 2001, Bono spoke over the newly

WALK ON

15

included *hallelujahs* on the emotionallyl charged climax, "I'll see you when I get home"—an obvious reference to eternal hope even in the midst of mourning. The evangelical Christian roots from which Bono, Larry and The Edge came have a core belief that heaven is only achievable by belief. A new millennium, Jubilee 2000 and the loss of INXS singer Michael Hutchence may have brought a few spiritual issues to the forefront of the band's thinking. It was time to take stock and ask some serious questions. What goes in the suitcase, and what has to be left behind? What are the important things in life? What are the transitory things? What can last the journey? What is of the moment? These spiritual questions are an ongoing theme of the Bible.

Ecclesiastes has a basic thesis of "everything under the sun is transitory and is meaningless" (Eccles. 1:2). Only a connection with God brings any sense to the meanderings of humankind. Jesus encourages His followers to forget about the treasures of earth because they get stolen or rust or moths eat them up. Treasures in heaven are lasting. The apostle Paul tells the early believers to put their trust not in things that cannot be seen because they are temporary, but to trust in things that cannot be seen because they are eternal.

At the end of the song, Bono lists the things that can be left behind: "*All that you fashion/ All that you make/ All that you build/ All that you break/ All that you measure/ All that you steal/ All this you can leave behind.*" They are man-made things, but he adds to the list all the wrong things or mistakes that the Gospel deals with. Jesus came and died and was raised to life to offer a new start, leaving the regretful things and guilt behind and heading on afresh. The song and the Gospel have the same conclusions: "*Love is not the easy thing/ The only bag-gage you can bring…*" Jesus, when asked what the most impor-tant commandment was, told the enquirer, "Love the Lord your God with all your heart and with all your soul and with all your mind and with all your strength. The second is this: Love your neighbor as yourself." Whether you're heading for justice on earth or a fuller realization of the Kingdom of God in the next life, everything else can be left behind.

The soulful, Motown-sounding "Stuck in a Moment," which may become a U2 classic, was written about the suicide of Michael Hutchence, an event that hit Bono hard. He claims that the song is an angry conversation between him and his dead friend." [12] Yet the title itself is another moment when the transcendent belief at the core of U2, and indeed this album, suggests that there is more to this whole charade than the material world or the clock that seems to hem us in like walls to our left and right. It is so easy to get stuck in the moment of our troubled and hassled and painful and angry lives. But there is the hope of escape. If we could lift ourselves out of the moment and see all our moments from a panorama above us, then this moment in which we are trapped would hold new perspective. Ecclesiastes deals with this concept as well. There is nothing new under the sun, and if there is nothing above the sun, then this is all "meaningless, utterly meaningless" (Eccles. 1:2, 9). But if there is something above the sun, then a different perspective comes to bear. That faith per-spective, a belief in an eternal God, gives hope and strength in the moment to keep on keeping on, and the conclusion of the song almost becomes a brother of "I Still Haven't Found What I'm Looking For": "*And if the night runs over/ And if the day won't last/ And if your way should falter/ It's just a moment/ It will pass.*"

"Elevation," which follows "Stuck in a Moment," is the song that would have sat most comfortably alongside the *Pop* material. From being stuck in that moment, it prays for elevation that would give a higher perspective: "*Love lift me out of these blues/ Won't you tell me something true/ I believe in you.*" Becoming the title of the tour to follow, "Elevation," like many songs on the tour, would take on a spiritual gospel feel. The "you" clearly becomes God. Elevation is about revelation and in the power of the live show touches close to transfiguration, a mystical experience that Jesus shared with a few of his disciples on a mountainside.

"Kite" seems to be Bono the magpie at work again, picking up scraps of thoughts and ideas and weaving them into another song of a hundred angles. From flying kites on Killiney Hill with his daughters, Eve and Jordan, to thinking about all that this world might throw at you like an unseen wind, this is a meditation on dying and pondering on whether we live life to its fullest. During a gig in Manchester, England, in August 2001, Bono dedicated the song to his father, who was dying of cancer and had just a few days to live. "I wrote this for my kids, but now I feel like he wrote it for me."

There is an overriding thought from John 3:8, where Jesus tells Nicodemus that the wind blows wherever it pleases; no one sees where it comes from or where it is going. Jesus was referring to the believer in that conversation, but that's the root of Bono's idea. Like a kite blowing about in the spirit unseen. This might be a moment when he is meditating on who his children will become in this unpredictable world and asking himself what they think of their father up until recently dressing up in makeup and horns in front of thousands of people every night.

"In a Little While" is about journeying home, and in this home, the singer will no longer be "blown by every breeze." There is autobiographical information in it. Bono seems to look back at his love with Ali and that line that harks back to the early days of U2 when it lived this tension between Lypton Village, the world of rock music and the Shalom fellowship: "*Friday night running to Sunday on my knees.*" On the Elevation tour, after the death of punk rocker Joey Ramone, the song took a new turn. Apparently, Ramone was listening to this song at the end of his battle with cancer. Bono prefaced the song by telling the crowd: "He turned this song about a hangover into a gospel song. That's how cool Joey Ramone is."

"When I Look at the World" is one man's desire to have a mind like Jesus. It is full of U2 honesty in that it speaks with Jesus about the difficulties of acting like Jesus in every situation. The song starts out as an affirmation of how Jesus changes the singer's life, then it addresses the struggle: "*So I try to be like you/ Try to feel it like you do/ But without you it's no use/ I can't see what you see/ When I look at the world.*" It is about trying—and struggling—to see the events of "Peace on Earth" from the other side of his dialogue with God.

"Grace" is an epic end to *All That You Can't Leave Behind*. It is an atmospheric ballad in the tradition of "One" or "With or Without You," but is more like "40" or "MLK." The ethereal mood is topped with the most beautiful poetry that evokes the grace of that word's other definition: "*Grace/ She carries the world on her hips/ No champagne flute on her lips/ No twirls or skips between her fingertips/ She carries a world in perfect condition."*

In a world where the eastern religions get a great deal more acceptance on the scale of cool than Christianity usually receives, Bono pulls a subtle little punch for the Christian belief in salvation by singing: "*She travels outside of karma/ She travels outside of karma.*" There is something about grace that makes even those who believe in it find it hard to believe in. You can hear the words and take hold of the understanding that here is an upside down world order where the first are last and the last are first and where acceptance is unmerited. In a world where the first are first, and the only way to be affirmed is to be the most intelligent or best-looking or most successful, it is hard to get reconditioned to the conditioning of grace. A flower doesn't bloom in one hour of sunlight, and a believer's soul needs constant exposure to the rays of grace day after day, year after year, before it moves from an intellectual assent to a truth that our lives bask in and live by.

The fact that the members of U2 were all about to hit forty in the year of their ninth album's release must also have led to some soul-searching. You can drift through your thirties without noticing that middle age is a whole lot closer than youth. That you are being adored by fifty thousand young rock fans every night, dressed up in all the latest fashions, and rocking and rolling can hold back such an awareness. But the band members' seeing themselves twenty years older than those at the top of the charts must have had its impact on where they should go next. Could they compete? Grace may have become a friend worth getting to know at this stage.

As they took to the stages of the world on the Elevation tour to promote *All That You Can't Leave Behind*, U2 was experiencing the unmerited favor of God. The band had not shown such a spiritual openness or intensity for many years. As it ended the show with "Walk On," Bono would shout, "Unto the Almighty, thank you! Unto the Almighty we thank you!" before leading the crowd in choruses of "Hallelujah!" When *Rolling Stone* caught up with Bono in Atlanta, he was open about what he thought was going on: "God is in the room, more than Elvis. It feels like there's a blessing on the band right now. People are saying they are feeling shivers—well, the band is as well. And I don't know what it is, but it feels like God walking through the room, and it feels like a blessing, and in the end, music is a kind of sacrament; it's not just about airplay or chart positions." [13]

WALK ON

15

GOD IS IN THE HOUSE

The members of U2 have been focused and clinical in their ambition to be the biggest band in the world. They've arguably been at the pinnacle of their profession for most of the past two decades, but Bono has never confined the meaning of his life to mere pop chart statistics. The music is simply the place where this Irishman makes rhyme and reason out of the big questions of life. Who are we? Why are we here? What has gone wrong? How can we put it right? For Bono it is about trying to find how a faith in God in a beautiful but sad and messed up world can work. He's a theologian, a social analyzer and political activist all rolled into one. Belief and activism are the things that drive him, and though the band may be less vocal they are happy to allow the front man to express their opinions.

In his graduation day speech at Harvard in June 2001, Bono was challenging and inspirational about the potential to change the world. Back in 1981, he said in U2's song "Rejoice," "*I can't change the world, but I can change the world in me."* U2 has seen the world since then and has come to dream the ideal that yes, the world can be changed, and these graduates from one of the world's most famous universities were not going to get off with a defeatist attitude. Bono wound up his speech saying: "We've got to follow through on our ideals, or we betray something at the heart of who we are. Outside these gates, and even within them, the culture of idealism is under siege beset by materialism and narcissism and all the other 'isms' of indifference." In general, materialism and narcissism are the very bedrock of rock 'n' roll— but not for Bono. Earlier in the speech, he defined rock as rebellion but then clearly defined the kind of rebellion that he was pontificating: "If I'm honest, I'm rebelling against my own indifference. I am rebelling against the idea that the world is the way the world is, and there's no damned thing I can do about it. So I'm trying to do some damned thing."

His speech gives us the honest and vulnerable Bono, the man who is prepared to rant and rave and allow his idealistic zeal take him across the lines of correctness and be accused of overdosing on sincerity or being foul-mouthed or idealistically naive. He is a man who, in the depth of his being, believes he cannot sit back and do nothing. Indeed he can do no other than give it everything, no matter what the consequences. The vociferousness of that—whether seen in his art, his politics, his faith or his life—often has received criticism from Christians thinking him too worldly and from the rock music press and fans for being too holy.

The complexities and spontaneous breakneck impulsiveness of U2's front man have fired what U2 is. That they were scruffily bound in a spiritual passion has given the band's blaze a unique twist and tale. When the Spirit Who roams his soul meets the adrenaline pumping feverishly in his red-blooded Irish veins, the fuse is lit to create an explosive live spectacular. But more than that, the fuse is lit to make him the hugest of rock personalities, not in any Jim Morrison-type, hedonistic, destructive way, but in a way that prods and provokes the entire world with alternative ways of living. As he said to the graduates: "Isn't 'Love Thy Neighbor' in the global village so inconvenient? God writes us these lines…we have to sing them…take them to the top of the charts, but it's not what the radio is playing, is it? I know."

Maybe it has been that subversive spirit, energized by the words of Jesus, that has kept U2 returning to the creative and commercial heights again and again. Maybe God is more obviously in the house than in that decade of horns and shades. But he has been on the lines and between the lines of U2's entire catalog, whether throwing beams of illumination across the band's study of the dark terrain of the modern world or shining brightly on albums such as *October* and *All That You Can't Leave Behind.*

The God dimension to U2 may be the reason why these guys stand unique in the realm of their chosen, or thrust-upon-them-like-a-gift-from-above, vocation. What other band is still producing anything as fresh and original twenty years into its career? What other band is giving the live act the kind of constant reinvention or passionate performance that U2 is doing? What other band is still living in the same place, with the same school friends? What other band has been able to maintain its sense of privacy and has given the press so little opportunity for tabloid headlines? What other band has added to its art the desire to use

WALK ON

16

its status to do more than make money and enjoy the fame? What other band has such a sense of vocation, a vocation that seeps through every pore of its recorded and live work?

As its Elevation tour rolls across America, Europe and the world, U2 is reaching out to a new generation of fans who are discovering the band's back catalog for the first time, sending albums

"I'm rebelling against my own indifference."

GOD IS IN THE HOUSE

such as *The Joshua Tree* back up album charts. And the members of U2 know now more than ever that nothing matters more than God's love and grace, which can change everything. It is intriguing that the openness of the band's faith has coincided with a return to the primary colors of rock that broke the band out of Dublin more than two decades ago. It is intriguing too that U2's return to some spiritual and political soapbox proclamation has been accepted whole-heartedly by the rock audience of the third millennium. The Church could almost pack up its contemporary music stall that it has resourced for forty years and head back home because on the Elevation tour, U2 has done what that industry has aimed to do—involve Jesus in the conversation of a generation. As the band's concerts finish with communal choruses of *hallelujah* just as they used to finish with Psalm 40, concert halls are taking on the spiritual feel and emotion of cathedrals and churches. God is in the house, and the world is there to meet with Him.

Chapter 2: Dublin City, Ireland

1. James Henke, "U2: Here Comes the 'Next Big Thing,' " *Rolling Stone*, 19 February 1981.
2. Niall Stokes, *Into the Heart* (London: Omnibus Press, 1996), 11.
3. Greg Kot, "U2 Renewed," *Chicago Tribune* (HYPERLINK "http://www.chicagotribune.com" www.chicagotribune.com), 2001.
4. Bill Graham, *Another Time, Another Place* (London: Mandarin Paperbacks, 1989), 24.
5. Ibid.
6. Os Guinness, *The Gravedigger File* (Hodder Christian Paperbacks, 1983), 82.
7. Howard Sounes, *Down the Highway: The Life of Bob Dylan* (London: Transworld Publishers, 2001), 323.
8. Derek Poole, "U2 Gloria in Rock 'N Roll," *Streams*, 1982.
9. Ibid.
10. John Waters, *Race of Angels* (Belfast: The Blackstaff Press, 1994), 154.
11. James Henke, "Blessed Are the Peacemakers," *Rolling Stone*, 9 June 1983.
12. Susan Black, *Bono in His Own Words* (London: Omnibus Press, 1997), 29.

Chapter 3: *October*

1. Neil McCormick, "Autumn Fire," *October Review, (Dublin) Hot Press*, 16 October 1981.
2. B.P. Fallon, *Far Away So Close* (London: Virgin Books, 1994), 47.
3. Bill Flanagan, *U2 at the End of the World* (London: Bantam Press, 1995), 45.
4. Mark Le Page, "Bass Notes: U2's Adam Clayton on Geography, Spirituality and Rock 'n Roll," *Montreal Gazette*, 26 May 2001.
5. John Waters, *Race of Angels* (Belfast: The Blackstaff Press, 1994), 168.
6. Liam Mackey, "I Still Haven't Found What I'm Looking For," *(Dublin) Hot Press*, December 1988.
7. Bill Flanagan, *U2 at the End of the World* (London: Bantam Press, 1995), 47.
8. Olaf Tyaransen, "U2: The Final Frontier," *(Dublin) Hot Press*, 8 November 2000.
9. Steve Taylor, *Youth Specialties Seminar*, Atlanta, Georgia.Chapter 3:

Chapter 4: "Sunday Bloody Sunday"

1. Niall Stokes and Bill Graham, "The World About Us," *(Dublin) Hot Press*, March 1987.
2. Susan McKay, *Northern Protestants: An Unsettled People* (Belfast: The Blackstaff Press, 2000), 16.
3. Liam Mackey, "I Still Haven't Found What I'm Looking For," *(Dublin) Hot Press*, December 1988.

Chapter 5: Live Aid
1. Chris Heath, "U2: Band of the Year," *Rolling Stone*, 15 January 2001.
2. Tony Campolo, *Who Switched the Price Tags?* (Waco, Texas: Word Inc., 1987), 23.
3. Robert Hillman, "At Home in Dublin," *Los Angeles Times*, April 1987.
4. Liam Mackey, "I Still Haven't Found What I'm Looking For," *(Dublin) Hot Press*, December 1988.

Chapter 6: For the Rev. Martin Luther King—Sing!
1. Bill Graham, *The Complete Guide to the Music of U2* (London: Omnibus Press, 1995), 38.
2. Ibid, 41.
3. Robert Hillman, "At Home in Dublin," *Los Angeles Times*, April 1987.
4. Liam Mackey, "I Still Haven't Found What I'm Looking For," *(Dublin) Hot Press*, December 1988.
5. Danny Eccleston, "The Elastic Bono Band," *Q*, November 2000.
6. Joe Jackson, "In Search of Elvis," *Irish Times*, 1 November 1994.
7. Peter Williams and Steve Turner, *Rattle and Hum: The Official Book of the U2 Movie* (London: Pyramid Books, 1988).
8. Steve Turner, *Hungry for Heaven* (Virgin Books, 1988).
9. David Breskin, "Bono: The Rolling Stone Interview," *Rolling Stone*, 8 October 1987.
10. John Waters, *Race of Angels* (Belfast: The Blackstaff Press, 1994), 165.

Chapter 7: You Know I Believe It
1. Niall Stokes, *Into the Heart* (London: Omnibus Press, 1996), 62.
2. Dave Tomlinson, *The Post-Evangelical* (London: Triangle, 1995), 3.
3. Robert Hillman, "At Home in Dublin," *Los Angeles Times*, April 1987.
4. Bill Graham, *The Complete Guide to the Music of U2* (London: Omnibus Press, 1995), 61.
5. "Top 100 Albums of the Eighties," *Rolling Stone*, 16 November 1989.
6. Niall Stokes, *Into the Heart* (London: Omnibus Press, 1996), 104.

Chapter 8: Heartland
1. Anthony DeCurtis, "Rattle and Hum Review," *Rolling Stone*, 17 November 1988.
2. Bono, "Remembering Allen," *Rolling Stone*, 29 May 1997.

Chapter 9: Reinvention
1. H.R. Rookmaker, *Modern Art and the Death of a Culture* (Leicester, England: InterVarsity Press, 1970), 30.
2. Steve Jelbert, *The (London) Independent*, 5 May 2000.
3. Bill Flanagan, *U2 at the End of the World* (London: Bantam Press, 1995), 207.
4. B.P. Fallon, *Far Away So Close* (London: Virgin Books, 1994), 47, 48.
5. Dylan, Bob, "God On Our Side," *Times They Are a Changing*. Columbia, 1963.
6. Brendan Kennelly, *The Book of Judas* (Newcastle Upon Tyne, England: Bloodaxe Books), 10.
7. David Fricke, "U2 Finds What It's Looking For," *Rolling Stone*, 1 October 1992.
8. Bill Flanagan, *U2: Complete Songs* (1999).

Chapter 10: Everything You Know Is Wrong

1. Achtung Baby, Island Visual Arts, 1992, videocassette.
2. Bill Flanagan, *U2 at the End of the World* (London: Bantam Press, 1995), 13.
3. Neil Postman, *Amusing Ourselves to Death* (New York: Viking Penguin, 1985), 3.
4. Douglas Coupland, *Polaroids From the Dead* (London: Flamingo, 1996) 112.
5. Achtung Baby, Island Visual Arts, 1992, videocassette.
6. Joe Jackson, "In Search of Elvis," *Irish Times*, 1 November 1994.
7. C.S. Lewis, *Of This and Other Worlds* (Fount Paperback), 73.
8. David Fricke, "The Wizards of Pop," *Rolling Stone*, 29 May 1997.
9. Joe Jackson, "In Search of Elvis," *Irish Times*, 1 November 1994.
10. C.S. Lewis, *The Screwtape Letters* (London and Glasgow: Fontana Books, 1955), 7.

Chapter 11: Midnight Is Where the Day Begins

1. Niall Stokes, *Into the Heart* (London: Omnibus Press, 1996), 120.
2. Douglas Coupland, *Life After God* (London: Simon and Shuster, 1994), 359.
3. Bill Flanagan, *U2 at the End of the World* (London: Bantam Press, 1995), 202.
4. Bill Flanagan, *U2 at the End of the World* (London: Bantam Press, 1995), 203.

Chapter 12: ...Under the Trash

1. Robert Hilburn, "Mysterious Ways," *Los Angeles Times*, 1 December 1996.
2. Ibid.
3. Stuart Bailie, "Pop Review," *Vox*, April 1997.
4. Joe Jackson, "Waiting For Beckett," *(Dublin) Hot Press*, 14 February 2001.
5. John Pareles, "Searching for a Sound to Bridge the Decades," *The New York Times*, 9 February 1997.
6. Jim Sullivan, "U2 Is Still U2 Even When Using the Tools of the Techno Trade," *The Boston Globe*, March 1997.
7. Mark Brown, "U2 Goes on a Successful Quest With Pop," *The Orange County (California) Register*, 2 March 1997.

Chapter 13: Wake Up Dead Man

1. John Waters, *Race of Angels* (Belfast: The Blackstaff Press, 1994), 1.
2. Bono, Introduction to *Pocket Canons* Psalms (Edinburgh, Scotland: Canongate Books, 1999), xi.
3. Ibid.
4. John Waters, *Race of Angels* (Belfast: The Blackstaff Press, 1994), 1.
5. Bono, Introduction to *Pocket Canons* Psalms (Edinburgh, Scotland: Canongate Books, 1999), xi.
6. Neil McCormick, "Growing Up With U2," *The Daily Telegraph*, 1 March 1997.

Chapter 14: Leap of Faith

1. "The Million Dollar Hotel press pack" Interference Web page, 1999.
2. Sean O'Hagan, "Billion Dollar Dreams," *Guardian Weekend*, 4 March 2000.
3. Peter Murphy, "The Million Dollar Man," *(Dublin) Hot Press*, 29 March 2000.
4. Sean O'Hagan, "Billion Dollar Dreams," *The (London) Guardian Weekend*, 4 March 2000.
5. Chris Heath, "U2: Band of the Year," *Rolling Stone*, 15 January 2001.

Chapter 15: Grace

1. Salman Rushdie, "Me Too," *(London) Sunday Times Culture*, 3 June 2001.
2. Aimee Mann, "4th of July," *Whatever*. Imago Recording Co., 1993.
3. Neil McCormick, "What Bob and Bono Did in Rome," *The (London) Daily Telegraph*, 1 October 1999.
4. John Leland, "Can Bono Save the Third World?" *Newsweek*, 1 February 2000.
5. Ibid.
6. Ibid.
7. Olaf Tyaransen, "U2: The Final Frontier," *(Dublin) Hot Press*, 8 November 2000.
8. Danny Eccleston, "The Elastic Bono Band," *Q*, November 2000.
9. Joe Jackson, "Waiting for Beckett," *(Dublin) Hot Press*, 14 February 2001.
10. Ibid.
11. Ibid.
12. Chris Heath, "U2: Band of the Year," *Rolling Stone*, 15 January 2001.
13. Chris Heath, "U2 Tour: From the Heart," *Rolling Stone*, 10 May 2001.

U2 SONGS CITED:

Boy, 1980:
Twilight
A Day Without Me
Ocean
I Will Follow

October, 1981:
With a Shout
Rejoice
Gloria
Tomorrow
October
Scarlet
I Fall Down
I Threw a Brick Through a Window
Is That All?
Stranger in a Strange Land

War, 1983:
Sunday Bloody Sunday
Seconds
New Year's Day
40
Two Hearts Beat As One

The Unforgettable Fire, 1984:
Pride (In the Name of Love)
Bad
MLK

The Joshua Tree, 1987:
Bullet the Blue Sky
With or Without You
Exit
One Tree Hill
In God's Country
Mothers of the Disappeared
Red Hill Mining Town
Running To Stand Still
I Still Haven't Found What I'm Looking For

Rattle and Hum, 1988:
All I Want Is You
God Part 2
Bullet the Blue Sky (live version)
Hawkmoon
Angel of Harlem
Love Rescue Me (U2/ Bob Dylan)
Desire
Van Diemen's Land
Love Comes to Town
All Along the Watchtower (Dylan)

Achtung Baby, 1991:
Acrobat
Ultra Violet (Light My Way)
The Fly
Zoo Station
Until the End of the World
One
Mysterious Ways
Love Is Blindness
Even Better Than The Real Thing

Zooropa, 1993:
Numb
Zooropa
Lemon
The Wanderer
Babyface
Stay (Far Away So Close)
Dirty Day
Daddy's Gonna Pay for Your Crashed Car
The First Time

Pop, 1997:
Wake Up Dead Man
Mofo

Last Night on Earth
The Playboy Mansion
Do You Feel Loved
Staring at the Sun
Please
If God Will Send His Angels
Discotheque

All That You Can't Leave Behind, 2000:
Peace on Earth
Beautiful Day
Grace
Walk On
Stuck In a Moment
Elevation
New York
Kite
In A Little While
When I Look At The World

Million Dollar Hotel, 2000:
Falling at Your Feet (Bono and Daniel Lanois)

OTHER U2 SONGS:

"Celebration," single, 1982
"Silver and Gold," *Sun City: Artists United Against Apartheid*, EMI, 1985
"Spanish Eyes," B side of "I Still Haven't Found What I'm Looking For," 1987
"Sweetest Thing," B side of "Where the Streets Have No Name," 1987
"Luminous Times (Hold on to Love)," B side of "With or Without You," 1987
"She's a Mystery to Me," unreleased, covered by Roy Orbison on *Mystery Girl*, 1989
"Slow Dancing," B side of "Stay (Far Away So Close)," 1993
"Hold Me Thrill Me Kiss Me," Batman Forever, Atlantic, 1995
"North and South of the River," B side of "Please," 1997
"Two Shots of Happy, One Shot of Sad," B side of "If God Will Send His Angels," 1997
"I Am Not Your Baby" (duet with Sinead O'Connor), for the movie *The End of Violence*

OTHER U2 ALBUMS:

Under a Blood Red Sky, 1983
The Best of 1980-1990, 1998

U2 VIDEOS CITED:

Achtung Baby
Popmart
Rattle and Hum
The Joshua Tree
Zoo TV

SONGS CITED (OTHER ARTISTS):

Band Aid, "Do They Know It's Christmas Time" (Geldof/ Ure), 1984.
The Beatles, "Helter Skelter" (Lennon/ McCartney), *The Beatles*. Apple Records, 1968.
The Beatles, "Don't Let Me Down" (Lennon/ McCartney), B side of "Let It Be." Apple, 1970.
Boomtown Rats, "Looking After Number 1" (Geldof), *Boomtown Rats*. Ensign, 1977.
Boomtown Rats, "Rat Trap" (Geldof). Ensign, 1978.
Browne, Jackson, "Running on Empty." Asylum, 1977.
Burnett, T-Bone, "Trap Door." Warner Brothers, 1982.
Burnett, T-Bone, "Proof Through the Night." Demon Records, 1983.
Burnett, T-Bone, "Having a Wonderful Time Wish You Were Her" (with Bono), *Behind the Trap Door*. Demon Records, 1984.
Burnett, T-Bone, "Purple Heart" (with Bono), *The Talking Animals*. CBS, 1988.
Cockburn, Bruce, "Lovers in a Dangerous Time," *Stealing Fire*. True North, 1984.
Cockburn, Bruce, "If I Had a Rocket Launcher," *Stealing Fire*. True North, 1984.
Delirious?, "Deeper" (Smith/ Garrard), *King of Fools*. Furious? Records, 1997.
Delirious?, "See the Star" (Smith/ Garrard), *Mezzamorphis*, Furious? Records, 1999.
Dylan, Bob, "Blowing in the Wind," *The Freewheelin' Bob Dylan*. CBS, 1963.
Dylan, Bob, "Leopard Skin Pillbox Hat," *Blonde and Blonde*. CBS, 1966.
Dylan, Bob, "All Along the Watchtower," *John Wesley Harding*. Columbia, 1968.
Dylan, Bob, "Blood on the Tracks." CBS, 1975.
Dylan, Bob, "Gonna Serve Somebody," *Slow Train Coming*. CBS, 1979.
Dylan, Bob, "Pressing On," *Saved*. CBS, 1980.
Dylan, Bob, "Every Grain of Sand," *Shot of Love*. Columbia, 1981.
Franklin, Kirk, "Lean on Me," *The Nu Nation Project*. Gospo Centric, 1998.
Friday, Gavin, "Each Man Kills Himself." Island, 1989.
Jean, Wyclef, "New Day." Columbia, 1999.
Lennon, John, "God," *Plastic Ono Band*. Apple Records, 1970.
Lennon, John, "Mother," *Plastic Ono Band*, Apple Records, 1970.
Lone Justice, "I Found Love" (McKee and Van Zandt), *Shelter*. Geffen, 1986.
McKee, Maria, "You Gotta Sin to Get Saved." Geffen, 1993.
Plastic Ono Band, "Give Peace a Chance" (Lennon/ McCartney). Apple, 1969.
Plastic Ono Band, "Luck of the Irish" (John and Yoko), *Some Time in New York City*. Apple, 1972.
Plastic Ono Band, "Angela" (John and Yoko), *Some Time in New York City*. Apple, 1972.
Plastic Ono Band, "Luck of the Irish" (John and Yoko), *Some Time in New York City*. Apple, 1972.

Plastic Ono Band, "Sunday Bloody Sunday" (John and Yoko), *Some Time in New York City*. Apple, 1972.
Plastic Ono Band, "Attica State" (John and Yoko), *Some Time in New York City*. Apple, 1972.
The Ramones, "I Remember You."
Simple Minds, "Sanctify Yourself" (Kerr), *Once Upon a Time*. Virgin, 1985.
Springsteen, Bruce. "No Surrender," *Born in the USA*. Sony, 1984.
Young, Neil, "Time Fades Away." Reprise, 1973.

OTHER ALBUMS CITED:

Delirious?, *King of Fools*. Furious? Records, 1997.
Delirious?, *Mezzamorphis*. Furious? Records, 1999.
Dylan, Bob, *Saved*. CBS, 1980.
Dylan, Bob, *Shot of Love*. CBS, 1981.
Moral Support, *Zionic Bonds*. Switch Records, Belfast, 1980.
Plastic Ono Band (John and Yoko), *Some Time in New York City*. Apple, 1972.

 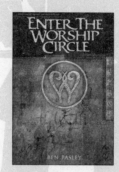